"Managing conflict is a skill, Lisa Gray teac
Healthy Couple; a skill we can learn to master. (
engaging as she guides the reader with examples and exercises.
book every client and therapist should have on their shelf."

—**Catherine Auman, LMFT**, psychotherapist, and award-winning author of *Shortcuts to Mindfulness*

"There are two things inevitable in life: Seasons of the year and arguments/fights with your spouse. Now you can do something constructive about inevitable disagreements. Causes and cures are at your fingertips. Follow the maps and find the treasure of conflict resolution. And just maybe, you can avoid the winter of discontent."

—**Peter Pearson, PhD**, cofounder of The Couples Institute, and trainer of couples therapists in sixty-six countries

"*Healthy Conflict, Happy Couple* is packed with real tools on how to thrive as a couple. Gray covers so much psychological understanding in an easily digestible manner. This book is a must-have for anyone who wants a more profound comprehension of their couple's dynamic, and actionable steps to make the relationship shimmer to new happiness levels."

—**Tasha Jackson (Fitzgerald), MA**, psychotherapist, widely published in magazines and on podcasts, and has gained national attention for her advocacy work and two TEDx talks

"No relationship grows without differences, disagreements, and fights; despite our best intentions. Lisa Gray shows us a compassionate and caring way to understand the conflicts with our loved ones, and disagreeing with our partners without losing ourselves or damaging our relationship. This is the book that anyone that wants to nourish a relationship and become the partner they wish to be needs to read."

—**Patricia E. Zurita Ona, PsyD**, author of *Acceptance and Commitment Therapy Skills for Perfectionism and High-Achieving Behaviors* and *Living Beyond OCD*

"The need to recognize and resolve conflict in a healthy, mutually affirming way is at the heart of Lisa Gray's book. Couples that fight together caringly can thrive. Many retreat from conflict or one person raises their voice, and unwittingly or otherwise, intimidates their partner and wonders about the stony silence or glossing of issues. This five-star book can bring the magic back into your relationship."

—**WJ Alladin, PsyD**, clinical director of the Centre for Couples, Narrative Coaching and Posttraumatic Stress in the UK; and founding editor in chief of *Counselling Psychology Quarterly*

"Lisa Gray has synthesized a practical framework and assemblage of tools for couples to embrace conflict as an essential skill in building lasting intimacy. Her approach is accessible, intelligent, and deliberate—and this book will prove to be a useful guide for couples willing to collaborate toward mutual understanding, validation, and ultimately, love."

—**Scott Spradlin**, professional counselor and lead therapist for the Wichita DBT Program at NorthStar Therapy in Wichita, KS; and author of *Don't Let Your Emotions Run Your Life*

HEALTHY CONFLICT

HAPPY COUPLE

How to Let Go of Blame and Grow Stronger Together

LISA GRAY, LMFT

New Harbinger Publications, Inc.

Publisher's Note

This publication is designed to provide accurate and authoritative information in regard to the subject matter covered. It is sold with the understanding that the publisher is not engaged in rendering psychological, financial, legal, or other professional services. If expert assistance or counseling is needed, the services of a competent professional should be sought.

NEW HARBINGER PUBLICATIONS is a registered trademark of New Harbinger Publications, Inc.

New Harbinger Publications is an employee-owned company.

New Harbinger Publications, Inc.
5674 Shattuck Avenue
Oakland, CA 94609
www.newharbinger.com

Cover design by Amy Daniel; Acquired by Georgia Kolias;
Edited by Brady Kahn

Library of Congress Cataloging-in-Publication Data

Names: Gray, Lisa (Licensed mental health professional), author.
Title: Healthy conflict, happy couple : how to let go of blame and grow stronger together / by Lisa Gray.
Description: Oakland, CA : New Harbinger Publications, [2023] | Includes bibliographical references.
Identifiers: LCCN 2023005921 | ISBN 9781648481697 (trade paperback)
Subjects: LCSH: Married people--Psychology. | Couples--Psychology. | Marital conflict. | Interpersonal conflict. | Interpersonal relations. | BISAC: FAMILY & RELATIONSHIPS / Marriage & Long-Term Relationships | PSYCHOLOGY / Psychotherapy / Couples & Family
Classification: LCC HQ734 .G7295 2023 | DDC 646.7/82--dc23/eng/20230209
LC record available at https://lccn.loc.gov/2023005921

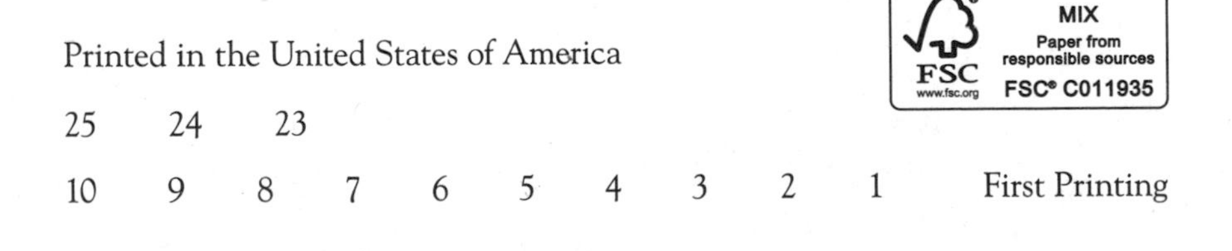

Printed in the United States of America

25 24 23

10 9 8 7 6 5 4 3 2 1 First Printing

Contents

Introduction

Toni and Joe shuffle into my office. They look scared, which is understandable. First sessions are so intimidating, and it's my job to make them comfortable yet productive. On their introductory questionnaires, they both said that their marriage is good. They just have one problem they haven't been able to solve, which is their different parenting styles. Joe thinks that Toni is a pushover and too lenient, and Toni thinks Joe is a drill sergeant. This should be fairly straightforward, I think. But when we start to discuss the problem, that's not how it goes.

"You let them do whatever they want! It's irresponsible!" says Joe.

"Irresponsible! You want to talk about irresponsible? How about that time that you spent money we didn't have on your precious car?" Toni explodes.

"Oh, you wanna talk about money, do you?" says Joe. "Let's talk about how many shoes you have in your closet!"

"And this is why I never want to have sex with you," Toni fires back.

Well, this can quickly get out of hand. This is what we therapists call *kitchen sink fighting*, a fight that starts with one topic but quickly dumps into the mix every issue going back for years. They'll just keep going with every complaint they've ever had if I don't stop them. But, of course, I do.

Sharon and Pete are a totally different story. Their questionnaires contained a host of complaints. Sharon hates how Pete is so stodgy, never deviating from his routine, and she said she feels bored. Pete feels like Sharon wants to just abandon the kids and go on luxury vacations they can't afford, and he's not that interested in going places with her anyway, because she's gained weight. And that's just the tip of the iceberg. We have a lot to unpack and discuss, and I plan for some intense sessions. But again, when we start to discuss the problem as a group, with everyone face-to-face, that's not how it goes.

"So how can I help your relationship? What would success in therapy look like?" I ask. Both of them hem and haw and mumble.

"Well, we'd be happier," Pete says.

"Yeah," says Sharon.

"Can each of you tell me one thing the other person could do that would make you happier?" I ask.

"Mmmm, I'm not sure," says Sharon.

"Me neither," says Pete.

Oh boy. These two were pretty clear on what's bothering them when they were filling out questionnaires, but then it appears they have nothing to say. Neither of them seems willing or prepared to discuss this in person. I feel like I'm working way too hard to get any traction.

Some couples blow up and escalate quickly, willing to yell about any perceived slight they have felt for the last twenty years. Other couples avoid conflict at all costs and can't seem to talk about anything of substance. These are two ends of a conflict continuum that I see, along with everything in between, in my therapy office.

If you're reading this book, I'm guessing that you are struggling with conflict, or with trying to resolve problems with someone important in your life, and you might not know where to turn. Wherever you fall in the conflict continuum, I can help you identify your conflict style and give you a road map for better resolutions. It may feel like a big challenge now, but by the end of this book you'll be armed with healthy strategies for managing conflict with much greater ease, and you'll feel much more comfortable in conversations that speak to the conflicts you and your partner typically have.

So what do I mean by a "road map"? In the beginning of a relationship, it's like the two of you are setting out on a journey with no destination. You aren't on a timetable, and you don't have anywhere you need to be, so you feel very in sync and things flow smoothly. It is very easy and natural. Who needs a map? But over time, you might diverge on what your goals are and how you should be getting there, or you may discover that your timetables for travel don't match. You start to feel differently about things that used to seem so simple. You have to decide which road you are taking and when and where to stop. And if only one person wants a change in the route, the whole thing shifts. By the time people come to see me, they're usually pretty out of sync. What we need to do is come up with a road map that works for both people, with clearly defined rules about what vehicle they are using, where they are going, and the roles they are both playing.

Unfortunately, one reason this can be so hard is that most of us never learned how to fight. Almost none of us ever had any kind of training or education in conflict management. We learned algebra and chemistry in high school or college, but no one ever taught us how to have good relationships—or if they did, it was a small unit among other topics in a health class. But relationships are widely accepted as the bedrock of satisfaction in life. Looking back on our lives, we aren't talking about professional success or achievements; it's our relationships that we value. They're the most important thing! And yet, no one ever taught us how to have good ones. What's more, the messages we do get about relationships don't always address the reality that conflict in relationships is inevitable—no two people will align perfectly in every respect and always get along—and that the key is not to be conflict-free or struggling through the same fights over and over but to know how to get through the conflict to the other side.

Many of the couples who come to my office tell me that they've been having the exact same fight, sometimes for years, with no resolution. And these are intelligent people! In my local area, we have lots of nationally known scientists; these people are working on quantum physics and such! And yet, for all their knowledge, they're still circling the drain with their partners, arguing over the same issue they've argued about for as long as they can remember.

The weird thing is, many of the problems these couples have are relatively easy to solve. It's not that the solution is so complex or unreachable but that they have never learned how to solve it. They either get distracted by a bunch of other complaints (like Toni and Joe) or they avoid the problem until it blows up like a volcano (which is what happens with Sharon and Pete). Or, they focus on the topic of their fights instead of the process of how they fight. But once they have someone help them with a road map to the landscape of conflict, a system for understanding what's actually happening when they fight, they can find resolution and be on their way.

I hope in this book to give you a clear, easy-to-follow road map to work through conflict. Using the strategies contained here, you may not be able to resolve every problem you have as a couple, but you'll be able to have more productive discussions in a friendlier, more collaborative manner and resolve at least some of them, and learn to fight for your relationship rather than against it. Doesn't that sound worth it?

How to Read This Book

I'm a big fan of books where you can just open to any page and find something useful. Unfortunately, this is not one of those books. Reading from beginning to end will be helpful, because the information builds on itself.

It will be difficult to follow later steps if you haven't absorbed what's been presented in earlier chapters.

Part 1 of this book introduces you to conflict styles and offers some tools to help you understand your own history with conflict. Unless you've learned formal conflict-resolution skills, your own conflict style will largely be a reflection of whatever you learned as a child, or in your formative years. Your conflict style will often operate in ways you can't quite control, because you don't actually know that you have one. The first part of the book will also help you cultivate the mindset you'll need to put the book's information to use. Some of the messages we received about conflict as children are just not useful or true, and we need to correct our thinking before we begin. I'll give you a list of things to avoid when fighting and some tips on how to do it. And lastly, part 1 will talk about managing overwhelm and your own body's responses to conflict. Conflict can trigger a fight-or-flight response, making us behave instinctively in ways that may keep the conflict going, so we need some tools to combat this.

Part 2 presents the road map for healthy conflict. It starts by exploring the setup for productive conflict and offers some tips for how to begin, which is crucial because conversations that don't begin on the right note often do not end with resolution. Part 2 then breaks down how to have a successful conflict conversation, covering all of the elements that make for good solutions to the problems we often navigate in relationships.

Throughout this book, I've included "client" stories to dramatize conflict in relationships. These stories are fictitious and don't represent any people I've worked with in my practice. Any resemblance to real clients is purely unintentional and not representative of our actual work.

Most of my clients rush too quickly into their own solution (yelling). Think about it: before you even enter an argument, you know what you want, right? You have a solution, and you probably think it's the best (and maybe the only) possible one! Because of this, couples don't spend enough time trying to really understand each other's position and brainstorming possibilities. So one strategy I always recommend to couples seeking to have productive conflicts rather than repetitive or constant ones is to break down the argument they're having into two conversations at two separate times. First you want to have a conversation in which the only goal is to gain an understanding of each other's position—no solutions allowed! Only after this has been accomplished can you have a second conversation focusing on problem-solving and solutions. This approach can be a challenge at first, but it really works. I can assure you that if you practice it long enough, you will be able to start moving toward having just one conversation, because you will have the skills to follow the road map, which will get you past unproductive diversions and toward the real heart of your disagreement. But for now, I'll teach you how to have two separate conflict conversations.

Part 3 covers some additional topics—the handful of topics, or buckets of content—that are typical grounds for arguments between couples. Here I will give you some specific examples of how arguments about these topics can be conducted and resolved. Then part 3 will help you troubleshoot the kind of conflicts you and your partner are getting into, and the struggles you might have practicing the skills in this book. From my own experience reading self-help books, I imagine you'll get to the end and still have questions. What about *this* situation? What if *that* happens? It is, of course, impossible to address every conceivable circumstance. But I will try to answer some of the more common questions and concerns that I've come across so that you can respond well to whatever comes your way.

Throughout this book, there will be exercises to do, and some free tools are also available at http://www.newharbinger.com/51697. I highly suggest that you pause to do the exercises. As we all know, conflict is difficult for most of us. Just reading about how to do it well isn't going to do the trick. I like to tell my clients that expecting them to handle conflict differently overnight would be like handing them a unicycle and telling them to go ride it around the courtyard. They wouldn't be able to do this at first! They could do it eventually, but they'd have to practice—and that means *on* the cycle. They'd have to fall and get back up. Learning how to handle conflict is a process that takes a lot of practice.

So get a notebook to do your exercises and respond to questions. And if you're reading this with a partner, make an agreement that you will do the exercises together. If you have a partner who is unwilling to read this book with you or who is just uninterested, commit yourself to trying some of my suggestions to see if you can change the conversation for the better.

Conflict Is a Skill

Many people tell me that they're just not good at conflict. Or they tell me, "I don't like conflict," and I just laugh. No one likes conflict! It's not our natural state to enjoy being in disagreement and at odds with people we care about. But while some people are by nature more patient or less impulsive, none of us is really born knowing how to get through conflict when it arises. Ultimately, conflict is a skill. And as such, it can be learned, just like any other thing we've learned in our lives. You don't have to like it—in fact, you can dislike it for the rest of your life! But you do have to get good at it. Because, as you'll learn in the chapters to come, healthy relationships actually require conflict to thrive, and if you want a healthy relationship, you will need to learn this skill. Think of it like going to the gym. When you first go, you can't lift much, and boy does it hurt! But over time, you can lift more and more, and you aren't even as sore as you once were. Conflict is like a muscle: the more you use it, the easier it will become. I promise.

I'll note that while much of this book will be written assuming a partnership of two people, the advice in this book is applicable to all types of relationships as well as to partners of all genders. It also doesn't have to be read by both you and your partner or partners. Sometimes a relationship that's in conflict can feel like a dance that's going wrong; you and your partner are missing steps or are out of sync with each other, and it just doesn't look or feel good.

Can you fix a dance with just one person trying? I believe you can, although there are some additional considerations. When one person changes a dance step, the dance has to change; there simply isn't a way for things to stay the same. If only one person is changing, though, they can expect some pushback, even if the old way of doing things wasn't working. However, if there is a firm, kind, and consistent invitation for the other person to join this new approach to conflict, they often will. It's true that sometimes they won't or can't, and then you can choose whether to stay or go. But if you can accept that sometimes you will be out of sync, you'll still have many more skills for the conversations that you *do* have. I'll talk about these specific considerations in later chapters.

Moving Forward

When Toni and Joe come in to see me now, we first talk about exactly what topic we are going to discuss and then move through the road map. We work to start the conversation about the conflict from a calm and grounded place, to move through the problems as problems, and to help Toni and Joe hear each other out—rather than jumping to "solutions." Premature problem-solving is really just each partner pushing for their own way, or getting stuck in blame and anger without a truly productive exchange of feelings and needs. Does that mean there aren't a hundred other topics or issues? No. But if we solve just this one, today, then we're one step closer to healing their relationship. When Sharon and Pete come in, we first center ourselves and commit to having a tough conversation. We might plan something for after the session to calm them following this discussion. And then we dive into the road map and they willingly address a problem.

Do you want to join these couples in learning how to have better conflicts in your relationship, conflicts that strengthen your relationship by helping you truly understand each other and work through tensions before they tear the relationship apart? Let's get started!

PART 1

Foundations for Healthy Conflict

CHAPTER 1

Why Your Childhood Is Important

Almost no one who comes to see me wants to talk about their childhood. I blame Dr. Phil and the rise of TV and online advice givers. People nowadays want concrete guidance, steps, and strategies. And that's not a problem! Except...we still have to talk about your childhood. Why? Well, if you think about it, your family of origin is where you learned almost everything. The same people who told you that 2 + 2 = 4 and the sky is blue also told you a lot of other things, some overt and some covert. They might have told you that you talk too much—they may have actually said this or they may have conveyed it with nonverbal cues that you became good at interpreting. Maybe they told you that you were worth a lot, or maybe they told you that you were worth nothing. You likely believed them, whatever they told you and in whatever ways, and that makes sense: these were the people shielding you from the big bad world. They had it together, as far as you knew, even if they really didn't.

It's beyond the scope of this book to tell you what to do with *all* the wrong messages you might have received in your upbringing, but here's where this book will help: to correct any wrong behaviors you've learned, directly or subtly, about fighting, conflict, and anger. When clients tell me that they never, ever saw their parents fight, I think, *Uh-oh, we have a lot of work to do!* because it often means that the conflicts their parents had just festered, unspoken and unaddressed, or perhaps there wasn't enough intimacy between their parents for there to be any fighting. Other people say their house was basically a knock-down, drag-out fight 24/7, which is also not good. In some cases, people tell me that their parents got along okay, but siblings or some other member of the family taunted or abused them and the parents did nothing to stop it.

Ultimately, even if you consciously know now that what you witnessed wasn't healthy, it's still likely all you know. Granted, maybe you've educated yourself a little about conflict over the years—you may have white-knuckled your way into doing something different with your partner—but you still find yourself falling back into old patterns from childhood when you get mad or stressed. It's time to take a closer look at some common conflict patterns, or *styles*, so you can begin to understand your own and your partner's styles and how they might be meshing—or clashing.

Conflict Styles

There are multiple opinions and labels for different conflict styles, but I prefer the Thomas–Kilmann Conflict Mode Instrument. Many resources talking about conflict limit the styles they cover to a simple dynamic of avoiding conflict or pursuing it, or establish conflict style based on personality or temperament. The Thomas–Kilmann five-style model is designed to account for all personality types. I also like it because some communication styles (such as *accommodating* or *compromising*) are generally seen as positive, but this model acknowledges how they also can be detrimental. As you read about the five conflict styles in the Thomas–Kilmann model, think about which of these you saw growing up from your caregivers, siblings, or friends—and which you exhibit.

Accommodating

The accommodating style means that you're always ceding your needs to the needs of others, basically always giving in. Imani remembers growing up in a traditional household where her dad worked long hours and came home grumpy and her mom was a traditional homemaker. Who knows how the dynamic began, but by the time Imani could observe it, it went something like this: Imani's dad would come home tired and irritable, and her mom would have dinner waiting. Sometimes she would ask her mom to intercede for her on something, to talk with her father on Imani's behalf. Mom would intend to have this conversation, but when she tried, the pushback from Dad was immediate and intense.

"Can't you see how tired I am? Everything I do is for you! And now you're complaining?" he would yell.

I bet you know what happened next. Yep, Mom would apologize, back off, give Dad a back rub—whatever would make him happier. And as a result, Imani has an image of her mom that becomes smaller and smaller over the years. Not physically, of course. But the more her dad got his needs met, the more unhappy her mom was.

You might empathize with Imani's struggles if you grew up in a home with a similar dynamic. Imani hated how her dad treated her mom, and she despised the weakness she saw in her mom. But whenever her boyfriend Bob comes on strong in an argument, she finds herself shrinking back. Her boyfriend—a pretty cool guy—is direct with his questions or statements about how he feels. He's not being hateful or mean; he's just really comfortable with conflict, and he's trying to have a dialogue. But there's something about the fact that she might be making him unhappy that Imani just can't stand. Because Imani's starting point is accommodation, I suggest working together with Bob to approach conflict in a way that Imani can initially feel comfortable responding to. With practice, Imani starts trying to assert her needs more. Bob doesn't yell or leave or insult her when she does this (as she has feared). In fact, he often is happy to accommodate *her*.

Avoiding

Avoidance is a pretty insidious conflict style and one which a lot of us saw modeled growing up. Mary remembers her mom standing over her dad yelling about a multitude of things while her dad didn't come out from behind his newspaper. People who avoid conflict often do it because their experience of conflict has been so uncomfortable. The way Mary's mom approached conflict surely didn't encourage her dad to put down his paper. He knew that Mary's mom would never be satisfied no matter what he said, so he didn't say anything! Mary also remembers her dad working in the garage or staying up late to make sure her mom was asleep before he went to bed. Over the years, Mary's mom gave up, as many people do when they're faced with a stone wall. These days, when Mary goes home, it feels like two people living parallel lives who have nothing to say to each other and almost no interaction. Nothing has been resolved, and neither of her parents is trying anymore.

Mary doesn't want to be like either of her parents. She wants to be able to calmly and effectively work through problems. However, she came to see me because her boyfriend Gerald has said he will leave if she keeps giving him the silent treatment when she's upset. She doesn't want to give him the silent treatment, but whenever he lodges some kind of a complaint, it just "shuts off a switch" inside her and she literally feels like she can't respond. I asked Mary if Gerald would be willing to come in with her, because she needs some supported practice at saying her truth and not having it come back to bite her. But even if Gerald won't come, I can help Mary start to approach conflict with other, less risky people in her life so that she can refine her skills before trying to practice them with Gerald.

Practicing with less risky people might look like telling the checker at the grocery store that you received the wrong change, telling the server at a restaurant that your food isn't quite right, or resolving a minor conflict with an acquaintance who isn't crucial to your life. As Mary works her way up to more important people in her life, she'll begin to trust herself to stay calm and clear during a conflict and begin to practice at home with Gerald.

Again, if you tend to avoid conflict, you probably learned it in your original childhood home, and the actual conflict you saw was probably unhealthy. Healthy conflict isn't horribly painful or intense, so there's no need to avoid it. In part 2, I will talk more about how to have healthy conflict, but for now let's continue with the conflict styles most of us learned as children.

Compromising

Compromisers are people who can see all sides of a situation and are willing to give up some of what they want for themselves in order to find solutions. I love compromisers. I'm sure we all do. Isn't compromising a good quality?

Let's ask Sharon. Sharon really gushes about her calm and healthy childhood. Sharon remembers her parents sitting at the kitchen table, talking very calmly and logically about every issue and coming to a compromise. But digging deeper, Sharon remembers a time when her mom really wanted a particular car. It wasn't a practical car, necessarily, but they had the money for it, and it was something her mom had always wanted. Sharon was doing her homework in the next room and remembers overhearing the discussion. Her dad made some really good points about how it wasn't really a family car. Mom wouldn't want dog hair in this nice car, would she? And what about taking Sharon and her friends places? Wouldn't it be better to have a seven-seater SUV that could hold all the kids? Sharon's mom admitted this was probably the case, and that's what they ended up doing. It was a super nice SUV with all the bells and whistles and, on the face of it, a good compromise.

However, talking about this conversation now, Sharon can see that her mom did not really get what she wanted at the time—and perhaps she never did. She made compromises for the right reasons, but Sharon can't remember a time—not even once—hearing either of her parents insisting on something. Everything was a compromise. There are times in life when we must craft a good compromise, but there are also times in life when there is something we really need or really want, and we must fight for it. If we're always compromising, we don't get the practice we need at honoring our own or others' desires just as they are. In fact, sometimes we end up losing any sense of what we want.

Sharon's husband gets frustrated because he can never get a handle on what she wants. He's a real direct guy, and he wants to make her happy; he just has no idea how to do it, because he can't figure out her preferences. Even going out to dinner, Sharon can't say, "I'm dying for Mexican food tonight!" Instead, it's always "I don't care, hon. What do you want?" That's nice. Sharon is nice! No one would say otherwise. But Sharon will never get what she really wants, because she'll never insist upon it. In fact, Sharon often doesn't even know what she wants.

Ultimately, a good compromise can be a useful tool. While there are times a good compromise can be a saving grace, if it's your forever style, you're never going to be really happy.

Collaborating

Collaborating is probably the healthiest style, if you're going to have a fixed communication style. Collaboration basically means that all parties in a conflict are trying to come up with a solution that suits everyone. Unlike a compromise, in the best-case scenario, you wouldn't have to give up anything; you'd be able to find a solution that both or all parties can really get behind. That said, while this seems like a conflict utopia, it doesn't always work that way.

June is a collaborator. She saw her parents do it as much as possible, and she does it in her work, helping to come up with solutions that work for both her coworkers and the clients. But now, June is stumped. She wants a baby and her boyfriend Juan doesn't. It's time for them to really come up with a solution, because June's clock is ticking. You can probably see the issue here: there's no way to collaborate on this particular matter. We spend a lot of time really discussing how they both feel: why she wants a child and why he doesn't. What it would look like if they had a child and what it would look like if they didn't. But there simply isn't a solution that will satisfy them both; one of them is going to get their way 100 percent of the time unless they break up and find other partners.

Collaboration is something to always shoot for, but in so many conflicts, it's a pipe dream. United Airlines and their flight attendants are never going to be 100 percent happy with the contract they hammer out; at a certain point, the needs and perspectives of owners and employees simply won't line up, so they'll have to settle for some sort of compromise. The key to figuring out if you can really collaborate is to get clear on what the ideal solution would be to each person. The classic guide to conflict resolution *Getting to Yes* suggests focusing on interests and exploring options (Fisher, Ury, and Patton 2011).

What happens most of the time is that we focus on our *positions*: I want a baby, and you don't. I want Mexican food, and you don't. The problem is that there are only two options: baby or no; Mexican food or no. If two people want different things, there is no way to collaborate. However, if you focus on your *interests*, more ideas can emerge. For example, why do you want a baby? When I asked June this, she said it's because she wants to have someone who will care about her when she's old. Juan wants this, too, but he has different ideas about how to get it.

We're making progress, because they both actually want the same thing, at least to some degree. The question remains, is a baby the only way (or the best way) to get what they both want? What are some other options? We talked about multiple ways their mutual desire could be met. June has some nieces whom she loves and who love her, which could provide some of the support she's looking for as she gets older. Juan enjoys multigenerational family gatherings and celebrations throughout the year, which could provide emotional support as June and Juan age. Either or both of them could do volunteer activities with young people. And so forth. There is no possible compromise on this issue—the two may still ultimately decide it is a deal breaker—but by focusing on their interests, instead of an either-or solution, we are able to find at least a collaborative attitude.

Competing

If you have a difficult person in your life or a narcissistic type, you probably have come across the competitive conflict style. Some people cannot or will not see another person's point of view but have a my-way-or-the-highway attitude. If you have two competitors in a relationship, things can really get thorny! More likely than not, relationships involve two different conflict styles. For example, Imani's mom would just back off and accommodate when her dad got into his competing mode. And when Mary's mom would yell about her needs, her dad just put the paper up a bit higher and avoided her. How can you possibly argue with someone who won't give an inch? But if you have two people who both insist on having things their way, explosions will occur.

Ariane and Michael are competitors like this, and no matter what I do, I can't seem to control our sessions together. It's a screaming match every time. They have competing interests, and neither is willing to collaborate or compromise. And they're definitely not yielding or avoiding the conflict. In chapter 10, we'll talk about dealing with difficult people in conflict, but I'll just give you a spoiler alert: it rarely goes well. For now, remember that you can't change other people, but you can always work on changing yourself and your style of communication and conflict.

Accommodating, avoiding, compromising, collaborating, and competing are not the only conflict styles out there, but one or more of these styles may correspond to how you or your partner fight as well as to how your parents or others around you fought when you were growing up. Ultimately, I like to think about these less as styles than as choices. Every conflict will be different, and it might be helpful to ask yourself what the best method would be in any particular conflict. If something is not important to you, maybe you'll just accommodate the other person. If you're not feeling good or you're hungry, maybe you will temporarily avoid a conflict, because it wouldn't be productive right now. You might be able to find a compromise you don't feel too bad about, or if you create enough options, you might even be able to collaborate on a solution you both love. And there are times when something is unacceptable and you are going to compete. For example, I am not going to collaborate on a solution when the other person wants something that is racist, harmful, or hurtful. I don't want to see their point of view, and I'm going to compete with it! So, as you can see, none of these styles are inherently bad or good; they are just tools and choices.

Now I'd like you to reflect on what you remember about the conflict in your home growing up, which will give you a better idea of what your conflict style might be. You'll want to have a notebook handy for this exercise so you can write your thoughts down.

EXERCISE: Reflecting on Conflict

First, find a comfortable spot and take a few deep breaths; perhaps close your eyes. Imagine yourself as a child, listening to some kind of a conflict your parents or caregivers are having. Where are you? What do you hear? Is it yelling? Silence? Calm conversation? How are you feeling inside as you listen to what is happening? Try to experience it not as you would now but as you would have experienced it then, as a child. Describe all of this in your notebook. Next, do you remember there being a solution to the conflict? Did your caregivers come to a compromise? Did they collaborate or did someone win? Write about this as well. Lastly, write down what you think your primary conflict style is and what you may have learned by watching your caregivers fight (or not).

Now that you've had an opportunity to look at your experience of conflict growing up and your conflict style today, it's time to move on to another big topic.

Let's Talk About Anger

Obviously, if you want to become more comfortable with conflict, you need to look at your relationship with anger. Conflict almost always comes about because something has made us angry. Okay, you can call it frustration or irritation or annoyance—but pretty much it's about some aspect or level of anger.

Anger is another thing that we learn about from our childhood experience—often negatively. I couldn't even count how many times someone, sitting in my office, starts talking about their discomfort with anger and explains it by saying something like "My dad was always angry" or "All my mom did was yell." Or maybe, rather than our parents, it was kids we knew in school who were bullies, or it was other experiences out in the world, like road rage. We have all seen destructive anger, and it's not pretty.

But anger in itself is not bad. Obviously, some bad behaviors come out of anger, but the feeling, the *emotion* of anger isn't bad. Anger is like a big, huge warning light that alerts us that something is not working for us; some boundary has been crossed. And that's good, right? If you never had anger, you'd just be a doormat, with no preferences and no hard lines that people couldn't cross. Acceptance and commitment therapy (ACT), a kind of behavioral therapy that's one of the foundations of this book, makes it clear that all emotions are okay, and that controlling, or trying to control, emotions never really works (that's the acceptance part!). It's only a commitment to behavior that really gets us where we want to go. It might be a big stretch for you to even think about, but learning to accept your feelings of anger is the first step toward controlling your angry behavior.

I'm pretty comfortable with anger, both my own and other people's. Working with high-conflict couples, there's a lot of angry energy that gets dispersed in my office. But whether it's a quiet, simmering rage or a knock-down, drag-out fight, not very many people are good at anger. Meaning, most people feel it and then expel it, either with words or behavior, without really even thinking about choosing what kind of response to have or what response would be most effective in their situation.

It's not a goal of this book to rid you of anger or to help you avoid feeling it. It's an emotion that will arise at points in your life, and as such, you must feel it. Instead, we are going to work on how to respond to it differently: to both your own feelings of anger and the experience of anger coming at you from another person. You can start by thinking about your own experiences with anger. Did you hear your parents or caregivers yelling when you were a child? Did they yell at you? If so, what was your response at the time? Did you hide? Did you yell back, and if so, were you punished? Or did you have a different experience as a child, perhaps where you knew one of your parents was angry but they didn't show it? Did anger ever come out in other ways? Try to make the connection between how you experienced anger and the way you display anger now. Some people just repeat whatever pattern of anger they saw, and others who try to go in the opposite direction often go too far.

Another thing about anger is that it's a *secondary* emotion. It's almost always paired with another, more primary emotion. For example, say your kid is out on a Friday night with a curfew of 11:00 p.m. The curfew time comes and goes, and no kid. You call, text, try whatever you can to reach them, but with no success. You are deathly afraid, picturing them in a ditch or hospital somewhere; you're almost in tears. And then, at 12:30 p.m., they come sauntering through the door like there's no problem. What do you do? If you're like most people, you get mad—really mad! But in this case, your anger is actually secondary to your fear. First, you felt deathly afraid, and your reaction to that fear was anger.

One of the first ways to work with your own anger is to understand, in any given situation, that anger is not everything that's present. If you can, try to figure out in the moment what other emotion is there, and speak to it. But even if you can't initially do this in the moment, you can always reflect on or journal about the situation later; you can try to determine what you were really feeling and if a different response—one that might have spoken to the other emotion—would have served you better.

Here are some other ideas for working with anger.

Understand Your Triggers

To become angry, there must be some kind of a trigger. Many times, when I ask my clients what the trigger was, they say they don't know, and it sometimes takes us a while to identify one. But there always is one, because anger doesn't come out of nowhere. Maybe you are just hungry, or "hangry" as the kids say. Or maybe you got angry when someone cut you off while driving. It would be easy to think that the trigger is the act of someone cutting you off, and that's one way of looking at it. But there's something deeper going on too. Did you feel disrespected? Offended? Having a good, comprehensive idea of the things that trigger your anger is helpful. You can then not only work to avoid those situations, if possible, but also be more prepared when you know a trigger is coming your way. For example, if you have a tendency toward road rage, and you know that it happens when you feel disrespected by other drivers, you can get in the right mindset before you pull away from the curb. You may still be triggered, but the more you know and the more you are prepared, the more likely you will be able to choose your own response—observing anger when it arises and then reminding yourself, *The other person is most likely in a hurry. Even if they are disrespecting others by cutting them off, it's not personal to me—it's their issue.*

Read Your Body's Cues

Anger almost always has a physical component. When I first start talking with someone who has anger management problems, they almost always say there is no space at all between the situation and their reaction—nothing in between. But when we slow it waaaay down and start to discuss their situations, then we can see that there's actually a lot more going on.

Zara has a boss who pushes her buttons all the time. She's coming to see me because her outbursts at work are unacceptable, and if she doesn't get a handle on them, she's going to get fired. Zara describes the situation as many people do: her boss "says that thing" or plops another project on her desk, and Zara just blows up, saying she "can't help it." I disagree! So to dissect it a little further, we look at a particular example of what triggers Zara. Yesterday, Zara's boss made an offhand comment about Zara taking too long on her lunch break, and Zara simply snapped, raising her voice in response. After talking about this situation, we realize some other emotions are paired with her anger. Zara often comes in early and leaves late, and her boss never gives her any kudos for this, so she's been feeling taken advantage of and unnoticed. This is a feeling she remembers having while growing up. Next, Zara realizes that she didn't sleep well the night before, and this was a trigger, because when she is tired, she has a hard time managing her emotions.

At first, Zara doesn't see any space where she could have responded differently in this situation. But when we start talking about her body, she realizes that when her boss started walking toward her desk, she felt her "stomach drop" and a ball of tension there. And when her boss started asking how long she had been gone for lunch, she felt a flush of red rising up from her chest to her neck. Zara realizes that these physical sensations often happen when she's about to blow. This is great information, because it means that when she feels her stomach drop or a flush occurring, she can see those things as an enormous warning light that she is about to be angry. Such body cues are different for everyone—I have heard everything from toes tingling to a tight chest to "hair standing on end"—but we all have them when we become angry. It will help to become aware of what your own bodily cues are so that you can have some warning that things are about to go south and you can choose other ways to respond.

Find Calming Techniques That Work

After becoming more aware of her bodily cues, Zara needs some techniques to manage what she's feeling before her anger explodes at work in ways she can't control. These techniques will need to be easy to do in public. We decide that as soon as Zara feels that feeling, she'll start to do some deep breathing. She'll also tap her legs with her hands—left, right, left, right. (*Bilateral tapping*, or tapping that goes from left to right or from right to left, is used in many trauma techniques and is a great way to bring calm.) Zara commits to taking at least one deep grounding breath—more if she can—anytime she feels her bodily cues. When becoming angry, this gives her the space to come up with some healthier responses, which will also help her stay employed.

There's literally no end to different ways of calming yourself down, and it's largely an experiment to find what works for you. Maybe it's walking around the block; taking a shower; listening to dance music; breathing. Whatever it is, it takes practice, practice, practice, because you're rewiring an old response with a new one. But with patience and persistence, it can be done.

Now take a moment to explore what you learned about anger when you were growing up, what you might have carried forward from that experience, and how you might become more aware of your own triggers, body cues, and calming tools. By doing so, you can create a different experience in the future, including with your partner.

EXERCISE: Your Experience with Anger

Get out your notebook and write about your childhood experience with anger. Try to recall a very specific incident where some kind of angry reaction was going on that did not feel healthy to you. Try putting yourself back in that situation and feel in your body the effect of this experience. Did you feel threatened? Afraid? Did you wish the people involved would stop yelling? Or was their behavior passive-aggressive, and you wished they would yell instead?

Next, once you have really imagined that situation, see if you can extract what lesson you learned about being angry. That you shouldn't be angry? That you should be? That only some people were allowed to be angry? That only some topics were worthy of anger?

And now write down some ways that you may have carried forward those lessons into your own life. In what situations do you get angry? How do you behave when you are feeling angry? Are you aware of what triggers the anger? Do you recognize other emotions that are present?

Lastly, come up with a list of things that you think might calm you down when you feel angry. It's best to make this list as comprehensive as you can, with ten to twenty options. Make sure that at least some of your calming techniques are ones that you can practice among people, in a crowd, or maybe at a family gathering. Here are some ideas.

- Taking five deep breaths
- Belly breathing, emphasizing the belly going up and down instead of the chest
- Alternate nostril breathing (videos can be found online)
- Bilateral tapping (such as left knee, then right, alternating) or any bilateral movement, such as snapping left fingers, then right

- Bi-aural beats, or music that alternates from left ear to right (available online; it's necessary to wear headphones or earbuds to get the full result)
- Walking around the block or getting outside
- Taking a shower (a cold shower can be especially invigorating)
- Taking a warm bath
- Putting your face in a bowl or sink of ice-cold water
- Listening to music and singing or dancing
- Doing a moving task, such as vacuuming or organizing
- Journaling
- Eating a healthy snack
- Drinking water
- Relaxing your muscles (progressive relaxation meditations are available online)
- Listening to a guided meditation (many free apps offer this)
- Playing with your pet
- Chewing gum (it sounds weird, but it can help to increase calm)
- Watching something funny either on TV or online
- Smelling something calming, like lavender, or any scent that you love

Feel free to use any of these suggestions, or come up with your own ideas. Write them down. Consider keeping your list in the notes section of your phone or somewhere else that's easily accessible.

When becoming angry, it can be hard to remember what you were going to do to calm down, so if you have it written down and kept it on hand, you can remind yourself quickly.

Moving Forward

In this chapter, you've learned about conflict styles and hopefully identified some of what you learned in childhood and how that has translated into your adult conflict style. This is helpful because, moving forward, you can pay special attention to the sections in this book that address skills that pertain to your particular challenges. You also learned how to recognize anger along with some new strategies to respond to it. Hopefully you've come up with some activities that will help you calm down when you get overwhelmed or angry.

The next chapter will introduce some mindset changes that will set you up for success when you and your partner are in conflict. I'm guessing you have had some negative associations with conflict, so I'm going to give you some new ways to view conflict in a more positive light!

CHAPTER 2

Attitude Is Everything

Like most people, you probably have some ideas and attitudes about conflict that are not helpful. The good news is that ideas and attitudes can change. My hope is that by the end of this chapter, you'll be able to see where your own may need to change and even make some progress. The first step is to get a clear picture of where you are right now. Think of this as the first half of a before-and-after exercise.

EXERCISE: Conflict Is…

Get out your notebook and fill in the blanks. Don't overthink it; just write whatever comes to mind when you read the first part of the sentence.

Conflict is…

Fighting leads to…

If we fight, we might…

People who fight…

It's a good idea to put off fighting because…

If I don't win a fight, …will happen.

If I tell you what I'm really thinking, then…

If we fight, people will think…

What attitude toward conflict do you think your responses to these prompts reveals? Maybe conflict makes you apprehensive because you and your partner or other people in your life have had so much of it. Or maybe your attitude toward conflict is a little defensive or aggressive; it feels like you have to win the fights you and your partner get into or otherwise, something bad will happen, even if you're not necessarily sure what that bad thing is.

I had an amusing experience when I first got married that may help to illustrate why I'm asking you to consider your attitude toward conflict. In my family growing up, we weren't exactly conflict avoidant, but we didn't have conflict very often, and when we did, it was painful and uncomfortable. I had also had a few romantic relationships that ended because of conflict, so I wasn't exactly a fan. My husband is the youngest of fourteen kids (yes, you read that right!), and early in our marriage, we went to visit his family. We were sitting around the long dining table in his dad's house with several of his siblings, and something sparked an argument between two of them. It wasn't anything personal—it was something about politics or a news item—but the conversation got pretty heated, or so it felt to me. I was like a spectator at a tennis match, looking to and fro, as the volleys shot back and forth. I must have looked alarmed. I certainly felt alarmed. Then, all of a sudden, one of the two brothers who had been arguing stood up and said, "Gotta go! That was so fun. Let's do it again!" My mouth fell open. I had never been around people who enjoyed that type of debate.

I learned an important lesson then: the attitude with which you view conflict will shape all of your conflicts. Back then, I certainly wouldn't have pursued any kind of conflict, but I also might not have responded to conflict or stood up for myself in a conflict unless it was truly "worth it." To me, conflict had been reserved for the worst-case scenario, and understandably so, since conflict had meant loss of relationships for me. If conflict for you has meant really brutal fights, weeks of silent treatment, or even the loss of a relationship, then you might feel similarly. And certainly, if you've ever been verbally or physically abused in a conflict, you'll be inclined to shy away.

Before we go any further, a word about abuse: abusive relationships, both physical and emotional, are beyond the scope of this book. The type of conflict that I'm advocating will not work with an abusive person, who by definition cannot have healthy conflict. If you're in an abusive relationship—meaning a relationship in which your partner mistreats you verbally, emotionally, and/or physically in a bid to control, manipulate, or simply hurt you—I recommend the books *Escaping Emotional Abuse* by Beverly Engel (2020) or *The Emotionally Destructive Marriage* by Leslie Vernick (2013). Or call your local help line or shelters for some specific, concrete assistance. This does not mean that you can't benefit from the learnings in this book; some of the strategies we'll discuss may reduce conflict and therefore reduce abuse. But it should not be a substitute for getting real help in your situation. No one has the right to abuse or mistreat you. And if you're being abused and mistreated, you have every right to leave the relationship and take care of yourself; you deserve to be treated well.

Conflict Is Not Bad

Going forward, you need a positive attitude toward conflict, because shrinking back from it will create more conflict. How can this be, you say? If I avoid conflict, there's no conflict, right? No, actually that's wrong. Two graphs (in figures 1 and 2) show the difference between couples who classify themselves as "no conflict" and couples with conflict.

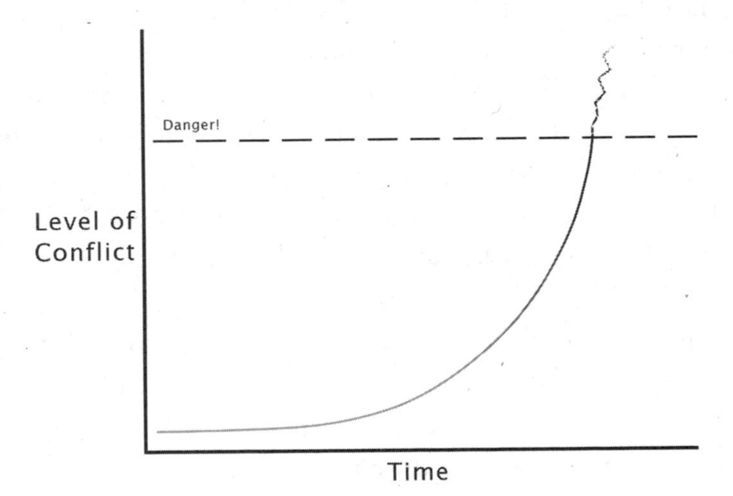

FIGURE 1. "No Conflict" Couple

You can see how there is no conflict, no conflict, no conflict—until there is a huge conflict, a possibly relationship-ending conflict. That's why almost all of us know couples who have broken up, and we were stunned. But they were so happy! They never fought. They got along so well! Actually, any two people on the planet when put together should have some differences. It's not that they had no conflict. It's that they never discussed the conflict—until they did—and then every single slight, no matter how small, was thrown in until it blew up the entire relationship.

In contrast, the next graph in figure 2 shows what a couple with conflict looks like.

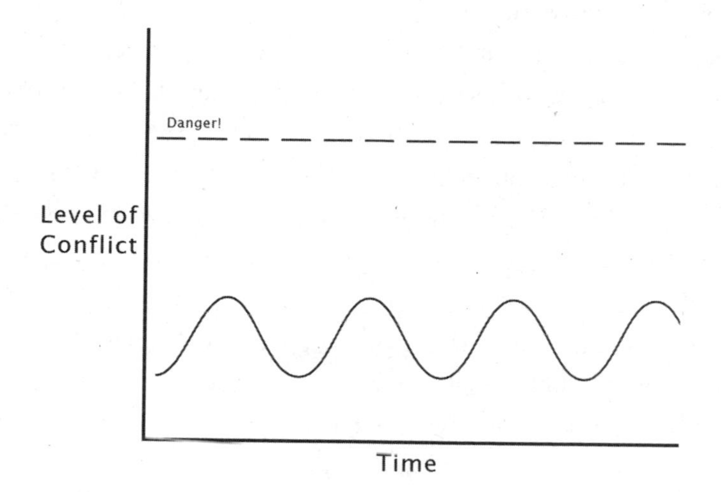

FIGURE 2. Couple with Conflict

What you see here is a lot of conflict, almost constant conflict. But it's low-level, brief, and resolvable. Hate the way they load the dishwasher? Talk about it. Thought they spent too much on those shoes? Talk about it. These are the happy couples. So, you can see that happy couples probably have more conflict overall than unhappy couples. It's just that happy couples address things that cause conflict at their lowest common denominator—the first time it happens—and they reach resolution then. Because of this, there never is a fight where things get thrown in from six months ago! Nor are there fights that reflect the simmering tension of so many previous conflicts gone unexplored, because there's nothing lingering around that long. The "no conflict" couples might look happy, but often their seeming lack of conflict comes from one partner or both partners suppressing what ought to be expressed or accommodating or compromising even when they feel it's unfair. There's a storm brewing just under the surface, waiting for the match and a spark. So can we agree that avoiding conflict actually creates bigger and more painful conflict?

It's like not paying off a credit card. You may be one of those rare people who pays off their credit every month, spending only what you can afford and receiving all kinds of rewards by paying no interest. The alternative is when you want something and think, "I'll figure it out later," then buy it and can't pay it off. Here comes the interest, and before you know it you're digging a hole you may never get out of. My point is, you can pay now or you can pay later; however, later is always more expensive and much less of what you really want in life ultimately. It didn't seem like that when you were buying those shoes, but that's how it works. Well, conflict is the same. Something crops up, and you're irritated, but you think, "We can talk about that later." Or one person says, "We should talk about this," and the other person says, "Can we do it later?" If you are like most couples, talking later never happens but the payment always comes due. You can pay it now or you can pay it later, but you are going to pay it, and later is always, always more expensive.

Here's another metaphor for approaching conflict. Have you ever been hiking up a hill or mountain, and the sky suddenly grows dark up ahead with an ominous-looking cloud in your path? Maybe the cloud is so close that you can't even see the trail. At this point, you could turn around and go back down the trail. But you were really hoping to catch that glorious view at the top, and you won't see it if you don't. So you keep walking. Pretty soon you realize that you are in the cloud, and as you walk in, it dissipates. You're aware of a cloud around you, but it's not as bad as you thought and you can see several steps ahead of you. Maybe it's even pretty. And you definitely get the view at the top. With conflict, many of us see it looming ahead and think, "No way am I going there." But actually, if you enter it—and I mean straight into it—you'll honestly find it's not as bad as you feared. You can walk through it and come out the other side just fine.

It's important to learn to approach conflict rather than to avoid it, because there isn't any way to have healthy and productive conflict if you're afraid of it. You might be asking, "But how? I don't want to pay now or walk right into it, so how can I change my mind?" You have a point: you can't just white-knuckle your way through it and pretend you believe something you don't believe. What you can do, for now, is trust that what I'm telling you is true, even if it doesn't feel true and even if you're feeling uncomfortable or afraid. Once you experience conflict as something you can approach, you'll know what I mean.

It might help to think of yourself as a pilot learning to fly with instruments. Pilots are taught to always, always trust their instruments, even if it's not what they feel is right while flying. For example, if you're in a plane that is upside down and you pull up, you'll feel like you are ascending when you are actually descending. The plane's instruments will give you an accurate picture of what the plane is doing, and even if it doesn't feel right, you have to trust the instruments to avoid crashing. Conflict is the same. If you are conflict avoidant, you are going to feel that having conflict is not a good idea—not now, and maybe not ever. These new mindsets about conflict are like your guiding instruments; you have to follow them and not the feelings. You must accept that conflict is positive and not follow the fear you might feel.

Cognitive behavioral therapy introduces various *thinking errors*. One of these is called *emotional reasoning*, which is the error of believing that because you feel something, it's the truth. Don't get me wrong, I respect and honor feelings! But what we feel is true is not necessarily true, so feelings don't have to control how we behave. For instance, I can feel like conflict is going to kill me, even if that's not actually the truth. I can also feel that what my partner did was done to intentionally hurt me, even if it's not necessarily true. The truth will never lead us astray, so let's fly by these new ways of thinking about conflict and not by how we feel.

Some other cognitive errors inform our problematic attitudes about conflict, so it's worth knowing about them, and how they might be present in your thinking, before you begin the work of change.

Cognitive Errors to Watch Out For

Here's a short description of some cognitive errors and how they might affect your attitude toward conflict.

Black-and-White Thinking

Black-and-white thinking, when you see something in all-or-nothing terms, is a cognitive error. It can play out with couples in conflict when they feel that what their partner did was 100 percent wrong and they pay no attention to whatever they did or said. I tell couples that I have been doing this work for twenty years, and no one yet has persuaded me that something is all one person's fault. Relationships simply don't work that way—they're interactional. Another way this can come up is thinking that your solution is perfect and that there is nothing good about your partner's point of view; or paying attention only to the ways your partner annoys you and forgetting their many good qualities.

Mental Filters

Using a *mental filter* means that when you take in information, you pay attention only to certain evidence and ignore the rest. This plays out in conflict when you zero in on one thing that happened but neglect to pay attention to all the contributing factors. I used to be an air traffic controller, and when I was investigating an aviation incident, what happened may initially have seemed clear. But in reality, investigators often discover a long chain of events that led up to the final activity. This is also true with conflict. Generally, conflict has many working parts, and paying attention to just one area will not give you the full picture.

Discounting the Positive

The meaning of *discounting the positive* should be pretty obvious. It's a common thinking error to home in on the negative and disregard anything positive that is happening. This isn't because we're terrible; it's actually biological. Our ancestors didn't remain in the gene pool because they stopped and smelled the flowers. They stayed alive by looking for lions and tigers! Our brains are wired to watch out for what might harm us, and the good slips away in the process. This hurts you in conflict because there are many wonderful things about your partner. Otherwise, you wouldn't have gotten together! But in a conflict, often you magnify the negative, which won't help you have the kind of attitude it takes to collaborate to reach a solution.

Mind Reading and Crystal Gazing

Mind reading is so common with couples. Maybe it started with all the fairy tales we were told as children, but there's an almost universal perception that if we love someone, we should know what they're thinking. In conflict, this is super problematic because we attribute all kinds of thoughts and feelings to the other person that may not exist at all! We also start thinking we can predict the future, also known as *crystal gazing*. We think, "I'm not going to talk to them about this, because they are just going to say x, y, or z." If this sounds like something you do, it would be good to cultivate a different attitude. Having the constant sense that you may not know what your partner is thinking (or what they may do next) may make you more curious, which will help you navigate conflict in a way that's healthy and strengthens your relationship.

Labeling

No one likes to be labeled, and this is something that will escalate into an argument nearly every time. If you say to me, "You're selfish," I almost have to argue with you! I can be selfish sometimes. We all can be. But if you label me as selfish in general, I'm going to push back, because it is simply not true. However, if instead, you say something more specific about the thing I did that seemed selfish, such as "I felt like it was selfish when you took the last cookie," it will be easier to respond. First, I wouldn't think you thought I was selfish all the time, and, honestly, if I heard my action described that way, I'd think eating the last cookie was selfish too!

In conflict, we often use labels to generalize something negative about our partner's behavior because we want our partner to see how much what they did hurt us. It doesn't feel as hurtful to talk about eating the last cookie, and it takes work to be specific about whatever is bothering us. But it won't help your conflict to generalize or label, and it may escalate the conflict to a new level.

EXERCISE: Consider Your Cognitive Errors

Journal about a time when you personally have used emotional reasoning, black-and-white thinking, mental filters, discounting the positive, mind reading and crystal gazing, or labeling when you were having an argument with someone. Write out the story of what happened. Now see if you can rewrite the story, correcting your cognitive error, and imagining how that person might have responded differently.

Next, journal about a time when someone has used one of these errors with you in an argument. Rewrite the story now, correcting the other person's cognitive error, and imagining how you would have responded to them differently.

Emotional reasoning, black-and-white thinking, mental filters, discounting the positive, mind reading and crystal gazing, and labeling are just some of the cognitive errors that might affect your conflicts as you go forward. Can you see how correcting these errors might really change the dynamic of your conflicts? I hope so.

Any Issue Can Be Solved

You might believe that conflict will solve nothing, but in truth, absolutely everything can be solved with a good conflict—not in the way you might think, though. There are actually two kinds of problems in relationships: solvable problems and perpetual ones (Gottman and Silver 2015). A solvable problem, for example, is "Should we get the Subaru or the Ford?" This is a solvable problem; you're going to ultimately end up with either the Subaru or the Ford or maybe some other compromise. Eventually with good communication, you can solve this problem and have a car. A perpetual problem is more like "I'm a spender and you're a saver." This problem is not ever going to be *solved* per se. I'm probably always going to be a spender, and you are probably always going to be a saver. Honestly, as much as couples come in wanting to absolutely change traits like this in their partners, it's just not going to happen.

The key here is the way in which each problem can be addressed. When it comes to the perpetual issues, the answer lies not in changing each other but in working together to find acceptable solutions to each instance in which the issue might come up. The issue could be a fundamental incompatibility in your baseline personalities, which can only ever change so much, or the ways each of you tends to express your personality. When people first come in with a perpetual issue, they are typically "against" each other, as you see in figure 3.

FIGURE 3. Me Against You

The solution lies in turning this around so that you're both facing the problem, like in figure 4. You fight the problem, not each other.

FIGURE 4. Us Against the Problem

So the new attitude is, "We can solve anything," not by changing the problem but by working together to find solutions that work for us.

All Problems Are Our Problems

Here's another poor attitude about conflict: "If I'm not unhappy with it, then it's not my problem." One time I saw an older couple who had been married for over forty years. The guy was simply fed up. So many years of silent treatments, fights, pleading, you name it. He was utterly unhappy. I listened to his story and got the picture. But when I turned to his wife to see what she had to say, she said, "I don't know what to say. I'm happy. This is *his* problem. Maybe he should come individually, because I've got nothing to do with this." She never came back, but he did, and they're unfortunately now divorced.

Here's the deal: relationships are a team sport. By definition, if one person in a relationship is unhappy, the relationship is an unhappy one. I believe what the wife said. She was happy. She had no issues with him. And that's perfectly fine, except that it wasn't enough to preserve the relationship. Because understand, folks, it takes at least two people to commit, but it takes only one person to get divorced or to separate. So if your partner is unhappy and you want to preserve the relationship, it is most certainly your problem too. The attitude to adopt here is "If one of us has a problem, we both have a problem."

Obviously, if you're the one with the "It's not my problem" attitude, then you can work on changing this mindset. But what if it's your partner who has that attitude? You may not be able to change your partner's mindset, but you can certainly bring their attention to the fact that they have it, and you can make conflict less awful and less painful by applying the concepts in this book. You may never change their attitude about whose problem this is, but if learning new conflict skills makes the partnership happier, that's your goal, right?

Conflict Strengthens Relationships

This chapter has covered the main attitudes toward conflict that I want you to have as you continue reading this book and begin applying the skills it offers. To really absorb the rest of this book and its information, it's crucial that you adopt these attitudes. Conflict might never be fun; it's not for most of us. But if you truly believe that facing it is better, that you can resolve anything, and that you're a team fighting against the problem, it's a very good start.

Remember how I said at the beginning of this chapter how appalled I was watching my husband's family? I didn't start out having these attitudes I'm espousing. My husband taught me. Early on, it would be obvious that I was upset about something, but I just wouldn't talk about it. This frustrated him, because it wasn't his mindset. He simply wouldn't tolerate it, and with patient cajoling, he would get us to talk about the issue. Because he had a healthy conflict model, we would resolve almost everything. I'd sit through our conversations scared to death, convinced that this might be the end. But a funny thing happened. Every time we resolved something, we got happier. Our relationship got better, not worse. The more I saw that heading into conflict brought me good things, the more willing I was to do it.

So, here's my last point, and it's a pretty hard one to believe: conflict increases intimacy exponentially. It doesn't seem like that could be true, but I'm living proof that it is. Being upset and not talking about it creates distance between people. In the old days, there were things about me—thoughts and feelings—that my partner didn't know. So how could you say we were intimate? We weren't! Yeah, we weren't fighting, but we certainly weren't as close as we could be. After the fight, he knew all my thoughts and feelings, and I knew his. Even on conflicts that we couldn't totally solve (I'm still a spender!), we at least knew enough to come up with solutions that might work for us both. We worked together.

So, again, don't be afraid of conflict. It won't tear apart your relationship or your life if you follow a healthy model for it. In fact, if you follow my road map, I'm guessing that a year from now you will have a closer and more satisfying relationship than ever.

EXERCISE: Revisiting Your Attitudes

Go back to your notebook. Now that you've read this chapter, try filling in these blanks again.

Conflict is...

Fighting leads to...

If we fight, we might...

People who fight...

It's a good idea to put off fighting because...

If I don't win a fight, ...will happen.

If I tell you what I'm thinking, then...

If we fight, people will think...

Are your answers different now? Are you surprised about how different your answers are?

You can take each of your answers and turn it into an affirmation to say on a regular basis. This will help you instill your new attitudes. So for example, if you now believe "Conflict is necessary," you would write an affirmation that's something like, "I will face conflict because it's necessary for happy relationships," and so forth. If you write an affirmation for each of your new statements, you may want to store them in your phone, in your notebook, or anywhere you'll see them regularly. Your brain listens to what you tell it, so even if these don't seem completely authentic now, the more you repeat these positive statements, the more likely you'll be able to act on them when conflict comes your way.

Moving Forward

You have learned the crucial attitudes that you need to progress in learning about conflict. If understanding or practicing these new attitudes feels like a stretch for you, I hope you'll trust me until you practice and see for yourself. You also learned about the cognitive errors that CBT teaches and how knowing about and changing them can positively affect your future conflicts.

The next chapter will move into active skills. You will learn some dos and don'ts for having a good conflict. While every couple may have their own unique rules for conflict, these are some universally important rules to put into place and agree on before you start practicing conflict.

CHAPTER 3

Dos and Don'ts

In Dan Wile's fantastic book *After the Fight*, he says this about communication rules: "When we look closely at the rules of good communication, we discover that they represent explicit instructions not to do what everyone does all the time. They are attempts to correct legislatively (i.e., by making a rule) what we do instinctively. The rules of good communication are utopian rules; no matter what we are told, when the crunch comes, we are going to do what these rules tell us we shouldn't do" (1995, p. 249).

Now, I love Dan Wile, but that sounds a little hopeless to me! So I'm going to argue with him a bit in this chapter. He does have a point when it comes to rules; even leading couples expert John Gottman says that while it's all well and good to have good rules for a fight, when things get heated, no one does them anyway! This has to do with our brain structure and fight-or-flight response. Even so, I still think it's good to have communication rules and dos and don'ts, and to know those rules as you're going into the change process. Why? Because if you don't have rules, how do you monitor or measure your behavior? I get that you won't always be able to follow the rules; there will inevitably be times you behave in ways you know you shouldn't, or react instinctively before the part of your brain that could've helped you act rationally has time to kick in. But it's only if you know the rules going in that you'll know when you fall short of them.

We all know that diets don't work. Often diets make things worse because of the rebound issue of chowing down after restricting myself and so forth. But does that mean that I shouldn't educate myself at all about healthy lifestyles? Does that mean I shouldn't try to follow a healthy diet in general, however I choose to define that? In other words, the fact that diets don't work is no reason to throw the "healthy living" baby out with the bathwater. And I don't think that Wile and Gottman are suggesting that we should have no rules when we fight, even though following rules is difficult. It's back to a mindset issue, like we talked about in the last chapter. It's good to know that diets can be destructive and why, and it's also good to educate myself about being healthy and doing my best. The key is knowing that I will not always be perfect and that I shouldn't behave as though I can and ought to be. When lapses happen, or when I struggle to eat the way I might like, I should be compassionate toward myself and try again. If I'm attempting to institute a change in my eating habits, or any habits, refusing to be compassionate with myself leads mainly to more poor choices in the future. It's the same with conflict.

So, as you read through the rules I'll outline, keep this in mind: understand the rules, do your best to employ them in your day-to-day life, and be compassionate with yourself in the moments you're not able to practice them. Because those moments will happen, as inevitably as conflict in your relationship will.

Don't Play the Blame Game

Jill and Philip come to see me because Philip had a short-lived affair and they want help restoring their marriage. Or at least that's what they say they want. But the conversations all seem to go like this:

"You're the one who slept with someone, Philip!"

"Oh yeah, well you practically made me do it since you won't ever have sex with me!"

It takes me a while to convince them that they can be mad and blame each other—they each have the right to do that—but if this is what they want to do, it's at odds with restoring their relationship. Just firing back what the other person did is unproductive. Not that it's unwarranted, but it's just unproductive.

Instead, we acknowledge that, yes, Philip did in fact sleep with someone else. This is not about neglecting an injury or a harm that was done: Jill's pain is real, and her anger at Philip is understandable; and Philip's behavior is something he will need to account and make amends for. But to really address the conflict, and make it productive and not destructive for the relationship, we want to drop down to a more vulnerable level. We want to deeply understand how this couple moved from their blissful wedding to this. How had they drifted apart? Why did they both feel so estranged from each other? If they can stop blaming each other, then Philip can gain a deeper understanding of why Jill doesn't want to have sex and why she didn't previously want to be close to him. Turns out, she feels pretty resentful of how things have gone since they had kids. Yes, she appreciates being able to stay at home, but she does all the housework and often feels like she has kids hanging on her all day long. The last thing she wants when Philip comes home is for someone else to touch her! She actually wants him to go away at those times—with the kids, please. I ask Philip if he can understand this, and he can. This isn't about sex, fundamentally. This is about an imbalance of duties and power, and just sheer exhaustion.

For Philip's part, he had so enjoyed the lightness of their life before kids, and he didn't even want that third child, whom he obviously loves now! He allowed his resentment to grow, and coming home started to be a drag. He knows that Jill resents that he gets to leave and go out into the world every day, but his job is exhausting too, and then he walks into chaos every single night. When his delightful coworker started chatting and spending more time hanging around his desk, it just felt so nice to be liked again. To feel charming and appreciated, something he no longer got at home.

This is such a common story. The thing that you can clearly see is that simply blaming each other did Jill and Philip absolutely no good. As I said before, relationships are interactional, so when things go wrong, we tend to blame the other person, but it's just impossible that it's 100 percent anyone's fault. After I got this couple to stop blaming each other, we made a lot more progress. They were each allowed to have strong feelings about what the other person had done, but they were more able to see how their own choices had also played into the end result. Again, to be clear, I'm not saying that the choice to have an affair is anyone else's responsibility or fault other than the person who made the choice and had the affair, but I am saying that it doesn't happen in a vacuum. Once this couple had a chance to talk through the affair—and the circumstances that led up to it—and take an honest, nondefensive look at where they both were now, Philip was able to make amends. He also really got how overwhelmed Jill was, and they were able to come up with a better system, including breaks for her, a better workload division, a great babysitter, and so on. Jill then had much more energy to be able to talk with Philip again and work to restore their intimacy. They never would have gotten there by just blaming each other.

Don't Need to Be Right

I'll never forget a workshop I went to where the speaker had a big stack of cards; half of them said "right" and half of them said "wrong." She had two people come up to argue about a certain topic, and at random times she would slap a card down and say, "That's right!" or "That's wrong!" Of course, we were all cracking up at the absurdity of it, but it was a demonstration of how useless it is to insist on things being right or wrong in an argument. There was really no logic or rhyme or reason to when she would declare things right or wrong, and that's often how I feel with couples in the therapy room.

Not that it seems absurd to them. They're absolutely convinced of their rightness, and they often want me to confirm that they're right and their partner is wrong:

> "Don't you think it's wrong for her to be friends with her ex-girlfriend?"
>
> "Isn't it bad when he won't come to my work parties with me?"
>
> "Tell her she is wrong to never let our kids have treats!"

And on and on. Most of the things that people insist are right or wrong actually have no clear answer. When something feels very wrong to you, it can seem like the other person is way out of line, but this is just another example of black-and-white, or all-or-nothing, thinking. Not that there aren't absolute truths. For example, murder is considered inherently wrong in every culture. But some people say the death penalty is horribly wrong, and others say it's right. Who is correct? Well, it depends. It depends on your history, your philosophies, and perhaps your religion.

Of course, the death penalty, along with many other issues we have strong feelings about, isn't often a matter about which we can be neutral. Sure, some of us will, when asked about it, be able to say, "Well, I think maybe this, but I could be wrong. I can also see the other side because of such-and-such." More often, it's "Yes, it's right" or "No, it's wrong." The side you're on is right, the other side is wrong, wrong, wrong, and there are no two ways about it. The problem when it comes to relationships is that if you need to be right, to have your position be the one that's agreed with and the one that rules the day, you stop listening to anyone else, period.

The antidote to needing to be right is developing acceptance of the other person's beliefs. Note that *acceptance* does not mean agreement. It just means accepting the facts of a situation (like the fact that your partner wants to be friends with her ex-girlfriend) for what they are, rather than resisting them or wishing they were different.

So I ask this couple, why does she want to be friends with her ex-girlfriend? And why exactly does this bother you? And so forth. My clients are always so disappointed when I won't make some firm blanket statement that they're simply right and their partner is simply wrong. I explain that intelligent, good people are allowed to disagree on issues and that our stances on issues are generally based on personal experiences. And I let them know that there's always a way to communicate with their partner that will allow them to understand each other's positions, genuinely, rather than simply staying entrenched in their own. Doing this can give them the ability to help them through the problem in a way that being fixated on being right—and being known as the one who's right—does not.

My grandma used to say, "You can be married, happy, or right, but you can only have two of them." Meaning, you can be married (or committed in whatever way) and happy, but you'll have to let go of being right. You can be committed and right, but you won't be happy. And you could be happy and right, but give up on being committed! We don't often look at it this way, but don't we all want to be in good relationships and happy? If so, we have to give up on being right all the time, and on being recognized as the right one who'll always get our way because we're right and it's justified. It doesn't work.

Don't Argue About How or When

One of the most common things that happens in couples therapy is that a session will get derailed by an argument about whether or not something happened or how it happened. For instance, John and Lisa want to talk about what happened when his mom came to stay that didn't work well for Lisa. John is setting up the story.

"So, then my mom arrived on Tuesday, and—"

"It wasn't Tuesday, it was Wednesday," says Lisa.

"No, it was definitely Tuesday because I was talking to her about the Monday Night Football game when I picked her up!" says John.

"Whatever. Go on," says Lisa.

"Anyway," John says sarcastically, "when my mom got to our house, she said that the dinner was burnt—"

"No, she didn't. She said it was tasteless," says Lisa.

It takes us half the session to get the story out because every single detail is an argument. Even worse are times when the story goes by the wayside entirely and the whole session is just a he said–she said on some insignificant detail.

I'm not saying that getting a story right is unimportant. But it's also true that our memory is faulty. That's why if three people see an accident, they'll all report something slightly different in their statements. They're not lying. They truly remember it differently or experienced it differently. In an article in *The Hill*, Marc Siegel writes: "Fear warps perception and heightens risk and fear memories may be altered and embellished each time they are retrieved and applied to new circumstances… Strong emotions affect how we remember. Fear or traumatic memories are more ingrained in our brains. But they are not always completely accurate, even if we are positive that they are" (2018).

In other words, when memories are being stored in the presence of strong emotions, they're not always stored accurately. I know this is hard to believe. If you can't trust your memories, what can you trust? But it's true that our memories can deceive us.

What's important is not whether or not you're right that your mother-in-law said your meal was "tasteless." What's important is how she made you feel. Your feelings are legitimate and important, and we can have a very fruitful discussion about them rather than arguing about whether or not something actually happened exactly the way you recall it.

Don't Argue When You're on Something

Years ago, I saw a couple who fought all of the time. Session after session we went over whatever huge fight had occurred that week. It took me a while to catch on, but eventually I realized that their arguments always happened when they had been drinking. So I asked, "What percentage of the time have you been drinking when you fight?" and the guy said, "Oh, one hundred percent." It was an important revelation. Now, when people I meet at parties ask me, "What's your number one piece of advice for couples?" I laugh and say, "Stop drinking!"

I'm no teetotaler. I like a glass of wine as much as anyone. But I can tell you this: I wouldn't trade anything of value to me for a glass of wine. It's a simple cost-benefit analysis. If you're losing anything—such as your ability to remember what happens to you, your ability to control what happens to you, or the security and integrity of your relationship—for the sake of a drink, that's a bad deal. It's especially bad if what you're losing is an important relationship.

If you want to use the advice in this book and have really healthy conflict, you're going to have to do it sober. Even one drink begins to alter judgment, reaction time, and emotions. And you are going to need all your wits about you to have a good argument. What's more, substances can often be a way for us to block ourselves from feelings we really need to be in touch with, if the goal is to have healthy conflicts and not unhealthy ones. I believe the reason a lot of people argue when they are using substances is that they've been avoiding conflict and suppressing things they're angry about. Once their inhibitions are taken off-line by alcohol or other drugs, here come all the complaints! The good news is that if you generally do not avoid conflict but meet your conflicts head on, nothing is likely to come up once you've had a drink! But even if something does, it's a really good idea to say, "I am kind of upset about this right now, but I know it's not a good idea to talk about it. Let's try to remember to discuss it tomorrow."

Don't Talk When You're Stressed Out

We normally operate from the front area of our brains with reason, logic, and thinking, but sometimes when we're feeling emotional or stressed out, other parts of the brain start piping in. When this happens, we are in the grip of more emotional, fight-or-flight parts of the brain, and the logical, reasonable parts of our brain become a little blurred, so we are not able to have a productive conversation. I'll talk in chapter 4 about stress and bodily reactions and how to manage them. For now, it will help to remember the acronym HALT, which stands for hungry, angry, lonely, or tired. Refrain from having difficult conversations when you are any one of these things!

Don't Be Defensive

Usually if we're in an argument with someone, it's because they didn't like something we did. None of us likes to feel guilty or be unable to explain why we did something, and we may get defensive. Defensiveness is one of four major barriers to good communication in relationships; the others are stonewalling, criticism, and contempt (Gottman and Silver 2015). Of these, defensiveness crops up most often in my office.

The problem with being defensive is that it derails the conversation. So if you say to your partner, "I cannot believe you just bought that couch without telling me!" then they will be likely to either distract you ("You bought a Kindle without asking me!") or defend themself ("You can't tell me what to do!"). Clearly this back-and-forth is unproductive.

Now, in the road map offered in this book, you would not begin the conversation the way I began that last one, with an accusation, which puts the other person on the defensive. Still, all of us will get defensive at times, when our partners say something that leaves us feeling accused or otherwise gets our hackles up. And there are some ways around this. Here are a few tips:

First, take a breath. Yep, just buy yourself a second or two by taking a breath. Maybe your partner will have moved on to the next thing, or maybe the oxygen in your brain will give you a different response.

Ask, "Can you tell me more about that?" I know, it seems counterintuitive to ask for more of what is already triggering you. But often we get defensive because we don't know enough about where someone is coming from or how they're feeling. And even if that's not the case, again you buy yourself a little time to decide how to respond.

My personal favorite is to pretend for a moment as though the person who is talking to me is really talking about someone else. I know it sounds weird, but I listen all day to people talking about what other people did and didn't do, and I never get defensive, because it's not about me, right? Similarly, when your friend complains all about what her partner did, you can listen without getting defensive, because it's not your problem.

I don't struggle as much with defensiveness now, but when I was trying to get better at it, and my husband lodged some complaint about something I had done, I would use this trick. For a few moments, I would pretend that he was talking about something someone else had done. This would give me a little bit of distance so that I could ask some good questions and get a better understanding. Then I could drop back into my own body, sadly realize he actually was talking about me, and deal with the situation in a better way.

Okay, that's it for the don'ts. Now I want to introduce some dos: some strategies to help you communicate well and effectively, especially when things are getting heated.

Do Speak from Your Own Point of View

One of those rules that Wile and Gottman say no one can do when they're angry is to use the old *I-statement*: "When you did this, I felt..." and so on. I-statements have become somewhat of a joke, but there's value to be found here. You don't have to begin with "I...," but it does help to talk about your own feelings instead of making an accusation about what your partner did. Using the example of labeling from chapter 2, if you say, "You're selfish. I can't believe you did that!", it's going to spark an argument. Again, the statement "You're selfish" is incendiary and untrue. It may be that your partner has done something selfish, but they are not all selfish. Anyone who hears themselves described this way is going to argue against it. You could say instead, "I was really hurt when you left me alone last night to go out with your friends. I thought that you knew I was sad about my dad being sick, and it felt selfish to me that you left." Saying this may very well spark an argument or a discussion, but you can see how it's just a lot easier for your partner, hearing this, to take in how you feel and own what they did.

Any statement that begins with "you" when you are upset probably isn't a good idea. When someone is coming at you, you basically have two choices: you can go right back at them, or you can disappear. If you start a sentence with "You are," "You did," or "You didn't," your partner will either meet you with the same ("Well, you are...") or simply disappear from the conversation by actually leaving the room or by checking out in their head (which is stonewalling). And you don't really want either of these responses when you have a complaint, do you? Most people will not meet vulnerability and openness—which are what I-statements often allow—with viciousness. So when you speak about how you felt and how you perceived what happened, most people are more amenable to coming your way.

Do Stay on Topic

There are certain times with clients when I become completely confused about what we are talking about. We start going in one direction and, before we know it, are talking about something else, and then something else, and so on. It's just impossible to solve problems this way, yet all too often, couples can get easily bogged down in kitchen sink fighting—you know, the kind of argument in which everything but the kitchen sink gets thrown in.

Imagine if you had a meeting on the job to solve a particular problem with others, and the meeting went something like this:

> "Okay, we are here to talk about the Jones contract and the issues we have with the graphics. Does anyone have any suggestions?"
>
> "Yeah, we need to use brighter colors. And we need to do that on the Smith project, too."
>
> "That Smith project is a mess. We are way over budget on that."
>
> "That's because you spent too much on research on that project. And Jessica doesn't even have any experience doing that level of research!"
>
> "Why did we hire Jessica anyway?"

Wouldn't this type of meeting be ridiculous? How would any project ever even get off the ground? The Smith project, the budget, and Jessica may all be legitimate concerns, but they're not the problem anyone is trying to solve right now.

Staying on topic can be difficult, because our brains are wired to "chunk" information for efficiency so we don't have to think about or figure out every single thing. For example, if I say "farm animals," you know I'm talking about horses, cows, pigs, and so on. I don't have to explain, "Now, a horse is a farm animal and a cow is a farm animal and a pig is a farm animal." It's brain shorthand, if you will. Likewise, if you're talking about what the Jones contract needs, and the Smith contract happens to need the same thing, it's going to pop into your mind. This is not a problem, as long as you have a plan to combat it, a way to bring the conversation back to the matter of the Jones contract, or stay on topic.

Moving back to relationships, let's say you are talking about finances with your partner, and the question of how much the kids' sports will cost comes up. That brings up the fact that your partner is the one who wants them to do every sport on earth, and you prefer that they do only one per season. This is a different topic—and it's one which the two of you often butt heads over—but if you start talking about it now, it will derail the finances conversation. My suggestion is to keep a notepad handy when you're having discussions. Whenever something you're talking about triggers thoughts about another related topic that needs to be discussed, simply jot down that topic on your notepad for a later discussion. You won't forget, because it's written down, which will allow you to stay on topic.

Do Give the Benefit of the Doubt

It's easy to forget when you're mad at someone that you love this person you are having some conflict with. They aren't a stranger to you. There was a time when you fell in love and each of you thought the other hung the moon. You would never have done anything that would intentionally hurt them! Now, though, it's easier and easier to ascribe negative intentions to what your partner is doing.

The thing is, almost everything that happens could be for a good reason or a bad reason; it just depends on your point of view. If you truly believe that your partner is trying to hurt you, then you'll absolutely ascribe a negative intention to whatever it is they did. However, if you truly believe that you are just trying to love each other and it's hard sometimes, that's different. In that case, if you're hurt by something your partner did, you're going to be more curious than mad. You'll think to yourself, *I know you aren't trying to hurt me, so why did you do that?* This sets you up to get more information, more background, and more of your partner's thoughts and feelings. It also sets up an environment where it's so much easier for your partner to say, "Oh, I'm so sorry!" than to get defensive. When you love one another, don't you think it works better if you assume that you aren't working against each other? As I tell my clients, if it becomes obvious that your partner does have malicious intent, that is an entirely different problem. But for now, let's assume that's not the case.

Lastly, Do Be Curious

My last piece of advice piggybacks on the previous suggestion. My goal in most of the conflicts that occur in my office is to slow things way, way down so that everyone can be curious about each part of the story. Because conflicts generally develop and then escalate so quickly, there's a lot you don't know, and won't know, unless you choose to be curious about what's driving them. I think curiosity is the most useful stance you can take in conflict. I cannot count the times, after slowing things down in my office, that someone will say something like, "Well, I didn't know you were starving when I took so long in the store!" or "I didn't know that you told your mom she needed to respect me more." If we had all the facts, I'm guessing about 80 percent of conflicts would never even gain traction. It's what we don't know that destroys us.

When our kids were little, sometimes my husband would discipline the boys, and I would be unclear on what he was trying to accomplish. Because I couldn't back him, I would stay out of it and let him handle it his way rather than be critical with "Why on earth did you yell at them like that?" (I yelled too, more often than I'd like to admit). Instead, I would wait a while until I could achieve a tone of true and pure friendship and then ask with curiosity, "Hey, earlier with the boys, what was it you were trying to accomplish? I really wanted to back you up, but I didn't understand what you were getting at." Either this would lead to a solid explanation, because my husband is a great dad, or he would say something like, "Man, I feel bad. I really blew that one" and tell me what he was trying to do. I can just tell you that neither of those things would have happened if I had popped off with the first option. Being curious allowed me to be a good support to my husband while getting great information so that I could be of help in accomplishing whatever the actual mission was.

Obviously, this is not an exhaustive list of dos and don'ts for conflict. There are as many rules as there are couples because we're all different. But if you adopt these basic rules, they will really help on the road ahead. Of course, you won't always be successful at following them, and I know some of the examples I gave here make it seem easy when it's clearly not. It takes loads of practice. Start practicing at times when you are not so mad and work your way up to times when you are a little more worked up. These rules will serve you well in every relationship you have.

EXERCISE: Applying the Rules

Get your notebook out and think about the dos and don'ts covered in this chapter. Which ones do you struggle with? Pick one that you tend to struggle with in a conflict and write about a particular time when it happened. Let's say you tend to get defensive. Think of a time when you got very defensive and write about what triggered you, why you got defensive, and how you responded when you did. Now rewrite the story imagining yourself being able not to be defensive. How would the story change? Do you see that there could have been a different outcome?

Or maybe you are traditionally not very curious in an argument. Write about the last time you made assumptions in an argument, or didn't ask good questions, and what the outcome was. Then rewrite the story imagining yourself being very curious, asking good questions. We don't know how the other person would have answered the questions, but if you know them well, you might be able to guess. What would have happened if you had been more curious?

You can try doing this rewrite technique for each of the do-and-don't rules that apply to you to help yourself visualize doing something different.

Moving Forward

At this point, you understand how your childhood contributed to your conflict style; you also have some new attitudes about conflict to consider and some concrete rules to follow to learn how to practice them. I've hammered away in the last two chapters on these attitudes and rules because if you don't adopt them, you'll be unable to follow the road map I'm providing in part 2. The road ahead will be clear enough, but your thinking will be too erroneous or your behavior too impulsive to follow the route. You can have a really great road map, but if you have oil in your gas tank, you're not going anywhere.

That said, right thinking isn't a magic bullet. When you're in an actual conflict, you also need to know how to calm down long enough to actually think things through and put your skills into practice. So the next chapter will introduce some brain science to help you understand why we behave the way we do in moments of conflict. I'm also going to give you some tips for calming yourself so you can actually do the dos you've learned without falling into the don'ts.

CHAPTER 4

You and Your Brain

The brain is an amazing organ. What we know about it is largely untapped, but more information is emerging all the time. One thing that we do know from neuroscience, the study of the brain, is that with some basic knowledge, we can find ways to control some of the brain's functions. This is important because, as we all know, it can feel like we're out of control in an argument.

So, let's talk about what you need to know when it comes to your brain! If you hated high school biology, no worries. I'm going to try to make this chapter as painless as possible, but it's really very important that you understand what's going on in your brain and your body during conflict.

The Parts of the Brain

The oldest part of your brain, or the first to develop, is the brain stem. This area operates without thought and controls automatic functions such as respiration and heart rate. Next comes your limbic system, which identifies threats and helps you react to stress or danger. Lastly, the cerebral cortex and frontal lobe control memory, language, logic, and empathy. Stan Tatkin, an amazing couples therapist who utilizes what he calls a "psychobiological" approach, calls the limbic system your "primitives" and your cerebral cortex your "ambassadors" (2012). Similarly, Rick Hanson, a psychologist who wrote *Buddha's Brain*, calls these areas the "wolves of hate" and the "wolves of love" (2009).

The limbic system isn't actually bad. We wouldn't still be in the gene pool if not for this area of the brain. Our limbic system constantly scans the environment for danger and helps us jump out of the way of a moving train or a hungry tiger. It's absolutely necessary to have a healthy, functioning limbic system. The problem is that sometimes the limbic system butts its head in where it doesn't belong, like in an argument with your spouse at the kitchen table! And unfortunately, it doesn't ask your permission before going into high gear. So, let's talk about what is going on in your brain when your limbic system is firing.

The first thing that happens is that the amygdala, which is continuously scanning for danger in the environment, picks up on a facial expression, a tone, body language, or some such thing and sounds an alarm. This kicks the hypothalamus into gear, and it directs the pituitary and adrenal glands to release cortisol and adrenaline. And now the brain makes a choice: fight, flight, or freeze. You've probably already heard the common phrase "fight or flight"; the third option is to freeze. With fight, flight, or freeze, your *dumb vagus* has kicked in (Porges 2011), and you may feel sluggish and uncommunicative for days. The dumb vagus is the evolutionarily older component of the vagus nerve, sometimes known as the *smart vagus*, which helps you downregulate stress.

The limbic system isn't concerned about reason, the logic of the situation, or any other details; it's only trying to keep you safe. It's why if you step off a curb and realize a car is bearing down on you, you aren't thinking, "I wonder if that's a Ford or a Chevy" or "I haven't seen that nice red color before." Nope, your limbic system kicks in to get you out of the way. Meanwhile, the other parts of your brain are offline.

This is why when my client Brad tells me he cannot control himself in an argument, I believe him. So when Brad's wife, Sara, starts coming at him about how he didn't pay the electric bill on time "again"—and what on earth is wrong with him?—Brad's logic, words, and reason go out the window. His limbic system has automatically kicked in. In Brad's particular case, he fights. He starts to yell back with everything he's got, everything he can ever think of that Sara has done, said, or implied that has hurt him. There's no productive problem-solving going on, because Brad isn't in the problem-solving, logical area of his brain. He is concerned only about staying alive. Of course, he's frustrated about his response—in retrospect he knows that he was not really in danger—but try telling Brad's brain that in the moment.

Of course, Brad could just as easily say "I'm out of here!" and walk out, slamming the door (flight) or stand there and say and do nothing at all while Sara rages (freeze). These three responses—fight, flight, or freeze—characterize the responses that many of us have when we feel threatened in an argument. Again, the process looks something like what's happening in figure 5.

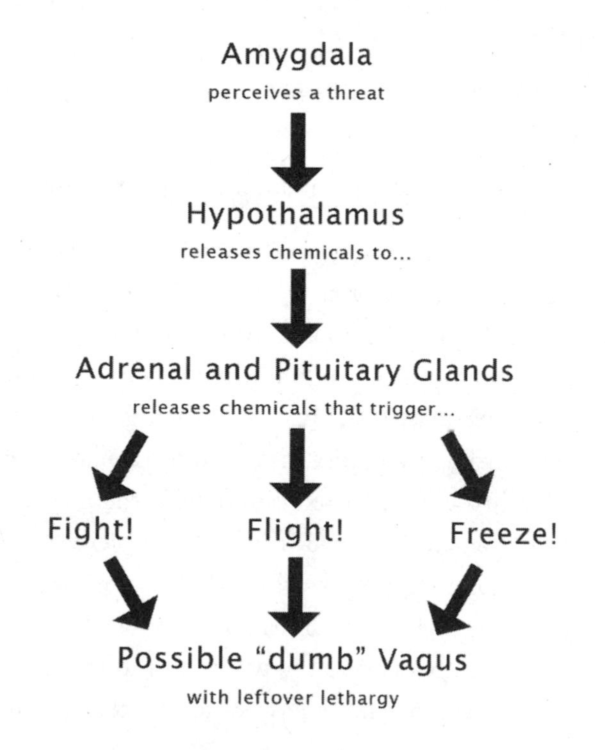

FIGURE 5. Fight, Flight, or Freeze Response

Now, obviously this is a simplistic explanation of what happens in your brain. Thankfully, we have other systems in our brain that can help us manage conflict, as long as we can keep them online. These are the "ambassadors" mentioned earlier: the helpful and diplomatic structures in the brain that keep the peace (Tatkin 2012).

The ambassadors don't operate in a cascade like the primitive system does. Rather, there are several players in the cerebral cortex, each of which has a different role to play:

- Smart vagus: calms cardiovascular and respiratory systems
- Hypothalamus: controls memory and antistress hormones
- Insula: gives awareness of bodily cues; controls attachment (our ability to bond with those we care for) and empathy
- Right brain: nonverbal; manages intuition, empathy, and body awareness
- Left brain: verbal; controls logic and processes detailed information, like words
- Orbitofrontal cortex: the moral and empathy center of the brain

When they're all fully online and functional, these systems of the brain work together, and the orbitofrontal cortex tells the other parts of the brain what to do, like the conductor of a well-trained orchestra. So how do you keep these systems online when it comes to conflict? In my view, figuring out how to activate the smart vagus is extremely important, because the more your respiratory and cardiovascular systems can stay calm, the less likely you'll get kicked into fight or flight.

Basically, we want to keep you in what Dan Siegel (2020) calls the "window of tolerance." In Siegel's theory, hyperarousal is when we're experiencing fight or flight; hypoarousal is when we freeze and are in a state of emotional numbness; and the window of tolerance is in between these two. When you're in your window of tolerance, your smart vagus is online and you're able to readily receive, integrate, and process information that is coming your way.

In the midst of a fight with your partner, your smart vagus is not online, and you're in fight, flight, or freeze mode. If you can stimulate the vagus nerve, however, it will counteract this process. There are several ways to do this, and there's only one catch: you must practice often and regularly enough to be able to easily access the vagus nerve when you most need it. Neuroscientist Carla Shatz coined the popular phrase "Neurons that fire together, wire together." This just means that if the brain does something often enough, it becomes paired information. If you want to be able to really use your vagus nerve to calm down when you're in a conflict, you'll need to start practicing some activities that will stimulate it and make these activities routine.

Here are some things you can do:

- Deep, slow belly breathing with a longer exhale than inhale
- Massage, particularly foot massage
- Laughter and social connection
- Cold-water face immersion (yep, just dunk your face in cold water!)
- Loud singing (finally an excuse to sing loudly wherever you go!)
- Yoga and meditation or prayer
- Taking a walk

Besides these activities, the skill of mindfulness will help you stay online in a conflict.

Mindfulness

Mindfulness is all the buzz these days, and there are many concrete and scientific benefits to doing it. Sometimes people have a strong reaction to the word "mindfulness," but honestly it just means paying attention to the present moment without judging what you're experiencing. Getting in the habit of practicing mindfulness on a regular basis will help you a great deal when you find yourself in a conflict.

Also, over time, regular mindfulness will lower your general set point for tipping over into a stressful state. Figure 6 illustrates this:

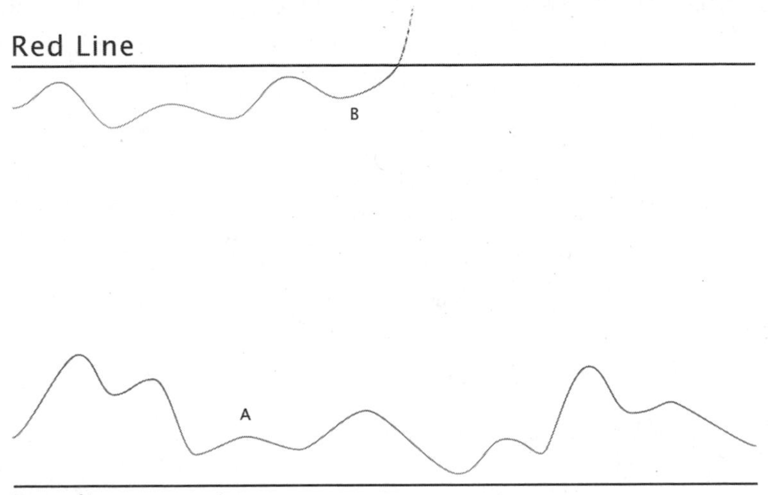

FIGURE 6. Lowering Your Stress Set Point

Consider the red line the point at which you tip over into fight-or-flight mode and the baseline a state of normalcy and calm. If you're walking around constantly living on line B in the figure, it's really only going to take one word, one eye roll, or one provocation for you to tip over the line. Mindfulness helps you live every day at line A, pretty much in a calm and peaceful state. Even if your partner comes right at you with some kind of complaint as soon as you walk in the door, you'll be close enough to your baseline, and aware enough of what might arise for you (anger, defensiveness, hurt) for it to take you much longer to cross your red line. Practicing mindfulness is an investment you can make in advance for healthier conflicts.

In acceptance and commitment therapy, mindfulness is put in different and equally useful terms. The acceptance component of ACT is to understand that feelings will come and go; that's the nature of feelings, and trying to get rid of them or change them isn't very productive. What is productive, however, is the commitment component of ACT: you commit to behaving in ways that will achieve your goals and help you live by your values in life. Viewed in this light, living at line A isn't about shoving your feelings aside or somehow figuring out a way to not let things bother you. Living at line A is about having a commitment to behaviors that will help you stay calm and live your life on your terms.

For me, the best way to be in a mindful state is to practice yoga, but there's no need for a formal yoga practice. Mindfulness can be achieved in everyday activities, though we generally don't practice it. For example, have you ever taken a walk and afterward someone asked you, "Was it a nice day out?" or "What did you see on your walk?" and you couldn't remember, because you weren't even present? If you were practicing mindfulness while walking, you'd be aware of everything in every moment. You would see the blue sky, hear the birds, feel the way your feet were landing on the pavement and the wind on your skin, smell the woodstove someone has going as you walk by, and so on. You would also be mindful of your internal sensations, thoughts, and reactions. Maybe you feel joy when you notice the blue sky, or you feel a little sad when you smell the woodstove because it reminds you of something. You don't get caught up in these feelings, but rather you just notice and observe them as if they were clouds moving through the sky or leaves passing by on a river. Over time, you get better and better at not responding or reacting to the emotional states within you, because you know they're continuously changing.

You can see how this would be a good thing, right? If you're consistently practicing mindfulness, you'll be able to observe and note the way your anger blooms in your chest as your partner meets you with a complaint as you walk through the door, but you won't necessarily feel like you have to respond right then. You might take a deep breath and say that you really want to talk about this but would appreciate just a moment to change clothes. You'd be able, while changing your clothes, to home in on what the complaint is, what your goal is for the conversation, and what you want to say or how you want to respond. Mindfulness offers you expert-level response management, but you do have to practice it to get there.

Later in the chapter, I'll give you several self-regulation exercises and talk more about mindfulness practice. But first I want to introduce another important tool to use when all else fails.

The Time-Out

It goes without saying that if you practice mindfulness and vagus nerve stimulation regularly, you'll get a lot better at self-regulation. However, we all know that nothing is effective 100 percent of the time. So, what can you do if you find yourself just completely overwhelmed and flooded during a conversation or conflict? Take a time-out.

Wait, aren't time-outs for two-year-olds? Well, yeah, and when your brain is in its fight-or-flight mode, that's basically what you are! Your centers of logic, reason, and language are offline, so your brain is basically having a tantrum. You need to put that brain in its place! And that's what a good time-out will do for you and your partner. The purpose of the time-out isn't to make your anger go away; the purpose is not to blow up. This is an example of what is known in ACT as a *committed action* that will help you achieve the relationship you really want.

Unfortunately, the mechanics of a good time-out are not usually intuitive to people, so let's go over how to make this strategy work for you. The very first thing you need is an agreement with your partner that you will use time-outs when you are overwhelmed. This agreement is best made in advance. If you don't have this conversation, and you simply yell during an argument, "I'm leaving!" or even "That's it. I'm taking a time-out!", I predict your partner won't let you do it. Why? Because if the two of you haven't agreed this is something you'll institute, taking a time-out will translate as "I'm never coming back to this conversation." You have to agree beforehand that it's unproductive to talk when you're not in contact with your cerebral cortex, and that nothing will ever get solved if you continue to do so. Then you have to agree on the process, or what happens after a time-out is called.

It's a good idea to talk about what will signal a time-out. Obviously, someone can just say, "Time-out!" but I don't recommend it. Often the conversation has gotten so heated by then that trying to verbalize anything may send the wrong message. Remember, the areas of your brain that regulate your tone, volume, facial expressions, and even language are offline at this point. Most of my clients come up with some sort of a hand signal (keep it clean, people!) like a "T" made with two hands, or really anything, as long as both parties agree that they understand the signal.

When one of you signals a time-out, you immediately separate and go into different spaces. You stay apart for a prescribed amount of time, and then meet back in the exact spot you were in before to continue the conversation. The reason most people won't let you exit a conversation is that they're afraid you'll never come back, so having a set time is helpful. When your partner knows you're coming back, they are much more likely to let you go.

So how long is enough time? Well, that's going to be a different answer for everyone, and it may be somewhat of an experiment to figure out. The answer is however long it takes you to calm down physiologically. In other words, it's not how long you want to avoid the conversation or how long it takes you to come up with an itemized list of ammunition for the coming conversation. No. Your aim is simply to exit fight-or-flight mode and reenter your cerebral cortex. In general, I recommend somewhere between twenty minutes and one hour. When you're in fight-or-flight mode, adrenaline and cortisol have been released; how long it takes to calm down will vary from person to person because everyone's metabolism is different. But whether it takes you an hour or only twenty minutes to calm down, do remember that the other person (the one who did not call the time-out) is likely anxious about the gap in time, and you don't want to make them suffer any more than necessary.

What should you do in this time-out? Again, the purpose is not to be in denial or to amass new arguments. It is solely to calm yourself down. Therefore, whatever works best to calm down your physiology is what you should do. If you don't know what that is, I suggest starting with the list of things I suggested earlier to jump-start the smart vagus. Things like a cold shower, singing a song, or even walking around the block to get some fresh air will help. However, try not to ruminate over either what has already been said or what you are going to say. This will keep you in a state of high alert and will not calm down your body. This is one area of life where distraction is a good thing and is what you're actually supposed to be doing. For me, singing "Late in the Evening" by Paul Simon is going to override anything else that's going on, in a good way. So find your go-to song or another activity that works for you. I have one client who likes to clean something during her time-outs. I don't get it, but, hey, whatever works for you!

At the end of whatever time you've agreed to, you meet back wherever you were when you parted. You check in with each other to make sure you feel calm and ready to continue the conversation. If not, you can extend the time-out or agree on another time to continue. If you're both feeling calm, you'll begin the conversation again (using the process that I'm going to outline in part 2). At a minimum, try to agree on what the problem is and the goal for the conversation before you start. You can take as many time-outs as needed, which may seem clunky, but it's so much better than talking from an overwhelmed state of mind.

Some of my clients really resist time-outs because they feel like it is "giving up" or "giving in." But it's actually a strategic retreat. A general in battle will sometimes pursue the enemy and sometimes retreat. When they retreat, it's not always because they are running away or being battered. Sometimes a retreat preserves the troops, or it allows them to come around another way or do a number of other things. In the end, a retreat—or a time-out—isn't about giving up or giving in; it's simply a strategy that makes your arguments more productive.

Remember Brad? Having committed to do a regular breathing exercise and practice mindfulness, plus join a yoga class each week, he's gotten quite good at managing his reactions and responses. Now he's acutely aware of what is happening. He's learned how to monitor and regulate his breathing when he and Sara are in the middle of a conflict; he can see when he's starting to become overwhelmed, ask for a moment to center himself, and take some deep breaths to keep himself calm. And in extreme situations, he can ask for a time-out so things don't get out of hand. He has a short yoga sequence that he practices while Sara goes to listen to some music, and then they resume. Note that Brad is not trying to avoid becoming overwhelmed. Because I've explained ACT to him, he knows that emotions come and go, just like waves or clouds in the sky. But he's gotten better at recognizing overwhelm, so he can execute his committed behaviors when that happens.

Breathing Exercises

I hope that knowing more about how your brain works will help you better understand what's happening in your body when you feel overwhelmed in an argument. Now I want to introduce some tools for self-regulation; these are exercises to do on an ongoing basis, to build skills and instincts that will help you when you're feeling overwhelmed in an argument. If you practice them regularly now, you can start making your conflicts more effective before you ever even get into an argument. Try them out to choose ones that work best for you, and then practice them regularly.

EXERCISE 1: Belly Breathing

Deep belly breathing is a tool that works really well, and you can use it wherever you are! Most of us, without realizing it, take shallow breaths, and belly breathing is different. It's simple, but it needs to be intentional. Put your hand on your stomach and breathe in deeply. While you breathe in, feel your belly inflating. Then exhale and pull your belly in as you do it. Breathe in and out like this ten times or as many times as it takes to feel calmer.

EXERCISE 2: Counting Breaths

Start with deep belly breathing. Now count the seconds of each inhale and each exhale, and try to make the exhale longer than the inhale. For example, breathe in and expand your belly while counting to four: one...two...three...four. Now exhale, pulling in your belly while counting to six: one...two...three...four... five...six. This timing works well for me, but you can modify the number of counts as you breathe in and out if you like. Ultimately, you want a full inhale, but you also want to take a second or two longer on the exhale. Again, breathe in and out like this about ten times.

EXERCISE 3: Box Breathing

The box breath is a simple breathing exercise that anyone can do. Breathe in for a count of four; at the top of the inhale, hold your breath for a count of four; now breathe out for a count of four, and hold your breath at the bottom of the exhale for four. That is one cycle. Note that you're spending an equal amount of time on each part of this exercise—inhale, hold, exhale, hold—like a "box." It doesn't have to be four seconds. Choose whatever amount of time works well for you. Do ten cycles of box breathing.

EXERCISE 4: Alternate Nostril Breathing

Put your hand up by your nose and hold your right nostril closed. Breathe in deeply and then out deeply using only your left nostril. Now switch your hand to hold your left nostril closed. Breathe in deeply and then out deeply using only your right nostril. That is one cycle. Do ten cycles of alternate nostril breathing.

This is one exercise you may not be able to do just anywhere, but it is very effective at calming the nervous system.

Choose one of these breathing exercises that you like doing, and commit to practicing it regularly, at least twice a day. I recommend doing it when you wake up and when you go to bed, or you can tie it to an activity that you always do so that it becomes a habit. For example, you could practice it in your morning shower and then before falling asleep. Again, getting into a regular habit of using your breath to calm you down will help this tool be accessible to you when you need it.

Practicing Mindfulness

Once again, mindfulness is the practice of paying attention in the present moment. There's no need to sit on a pillow and conduct a formal meditation practice, although that's certainly something you can do! Choose an activity that you'd like to do while practicing mindfulness: you might take a walk or practice it while you are cooking or gardening. Any activity will really work. Let's say you decide to take a walk. Pay attention to everything, and using your five senses is usually a good place to start. For instance, notice what you can feel: your feet as they fall on the sidewalk or trail, the odors you can smell, the colors and objects you are seeing. At some point, you may notice that you've started to daydream or that your mind has moved to random thoughts or worries. No problem! That's what our minds are designed to do. Just say, "Oh I'm thinking," and then let those thoughts go, and notice something that's happening in the moment—something you can smell, see, hear.

People often think they're not good at meditation or mindfulness because they notice that their thoughts wander. But they're wrong about that. Everyone's mind wanders. Mindfulness is a practice of continuously noticing when your thoughts wander and then coming back to the present moment. That your mind will wander is normal; it's what you do when you notice that it's happening that counts.

If you decide to practice mindfulness while cooking or gardening, it's the same basic principle. Notice what you can feel, notice the colors and items you are working with, notice if you can hear or smell anything. If you find your mind drifting, just calmly note that this is happening and come back to the moment. You can start with one cycle of practice per day, using whatever you happen to be doing as practice. If you do this often enough, pretty soon your whole life will be mindfulness; you'll be more present in whatever activity you do. This will be helpful when you are in conflict, because you'll be very aware of what's happening, both around you and within you. You'll start to notice an increased space between what someone said to you and your reaction to it. You'll know when there's overwhelm building in your body, and you'll be able to control yourself and the situation better.

Finally, a word on formal meditation. I do recommend giving this a shot if you're inclined, but it's easier to start with some kind of guidance. Many yoga studios have meditation classes; there are also many online tools and apps that can help you begin a guided practice of mindfulness.

Over the next week or so, try building a brief period of mindfulness and breathing practice into your daily routine. At the end of the first week, reflect: What was easy? What was hard? Note that you might need longer than a week's practice to start seeing real benefits, in terms of how easy it is to avoid getting activated in moments of stress. But often, even a week of consistent practice can be enough to begin getting the hang of the basics.

Moving Forward

Now that you know what's going on in your brain and how to keep yourself calm if you get worked up, it's time to move on to the actual road map for conflict. As with anything, the way you begin a project really matters. In the next chapter, you're going to learn how to set up your conflict conversations for success.

PART 2

Conflict Conversations

CHAPTER 5

The Setup

Most of the time, arguments simply erupt, bursting forth out of whatever is happening. But given how your body and brain work, you can see that letting arguments erupt isn't exactly the best way to do it. You aren't ready, there is no preparation—you may be hungry or tired—and you for sure are already mad. I joked before that I tell people who ask for my top advice that they should just stop drinking. My actual advice is to stop arguing when you're already mad!

If you've played golf, you know that the setup to a shot is very important: how your hands are placed on the clubs, the way your feet are placed, and so forth. Without a good setup, you won't be able to hit a fine shot even if you know how to play and have all the right equipment. It's the same with conflict. If you don't have a proper setup—a balanced mindset, an attitude of collaboration between you and your partner, and a relationship in which you're giving to each other even if there are conflicts between you that need resolution—it won't matter if you do everything else well. The setup is what puts you in a position to have a good conflict.

Should You Argue?

The first thing to ask yourself is, should you even argue? Now, I know I said earlier that happy couples have a lot more conflict, but it's at a lower level. For example, if you can successfully say, "Hey, babe, do you mind trying to remember to put the toilet seat down?" and your partner can say, "Oh, I'm sorry, I totally forgot, and I'll do a better job remembering," then you're done and it's barely even a blip. But happy couples also know the skill of choosing their battles; they know that some battles are just not worth it.

Here's a great statistic to keep in mind: happy couples have five happy interactions for each negative interaction, five compliments for every complaint, and so on (Gottman and Silver 2015). This 5:1 ratio is hard for most people to achieve, but it's a really good barometer to gauge how much you're arguing and how much you should be arguing. If you're very new at this, one way to keep track is to put five rubber bands on your right wrist. Every time something positive happens between you and your partner, move a rubber band to the left wrist. Until all five rubber bands are on your left wrist, you cannot yet afford to have a negative interaction. Now, obviously, this isn't how relationships usually work. Negative interactions don't just wait to occur until you have five positive ones! But chances are, keeping count this way will be an interesting way to see how often you're tempted to have a negative interaction and how often you have positive ones.

Another gauge I sometimes use is to simply notice the first time something irritates me but I don't say anything. Maybe my partner is just having a bad day, or maybe they are hungry or tired, so they're a little grumpy. I can let that go. However, if I notice that I am annoyed by the exact same thing a second time, it probably does need to be discussed.

Ultimately, you can think of relationships as an investment—there are withdrawals and there are deposits. When you first meet, you have a million dollars in the bank! There are occasionally withdrawals—maybe bad communication or an irritation—but it's no problem, because there are plenty of funds in the account to cover them. What happens for most couples is that, over time, there are more and more withdrawals and fewer and fewer deposits. By the time couples come to see me, they want to work only on the withdrawals, and I ask them how we can do that if there's no money in the bank to draw from. Not that we don't still work on the withdrawals, but I want at least an equal amount of time spent on making deposits.

When Chad and Sheila came to see me, they were overdrawn big-time. They sat as far away from each other as they could on the couch, arms folded and legs crossed, completely shut down. They spent a few minutes complaining about all the things that were wrong. I made the bank account analogy and shared my opinion that we really needed to start with making deposits. I asked them if they would be willing to talk for fifteen minutes a day, not about bills, the mortgage, kids' issues, or work, but just making friendly conversation. They were not interested. I then asked them if they would be willing to take a short walk through their vineyard each evening. Chad and Sheila run a small vineyard, with Chad working out in the field and Sheila doing the accounting and book-keeping. On these walks, they'd be holding hands to restore touch but not necessarily saying anything.

"No way," said Chad. "The last thing I want to do right now is touch."

Hmm. I made several other suggestions, but nothing met with a good reception. I reiterated that it would be a poor use of their time and resources to come in and complain if they weren't willing to do one positive thing for their relationship. When they walked out of the session, I was certain I would never see them again.

Imagine my surprise when they called midweek and asked to schedule another session. The couple that walked into my office the following week were like completely different people! Their body language was relaxed, they sat closer to each other, and they actually smiled.

"What happened this week?" I asked.

Chad piped in, "Well, I decided that I'd come home on time for a change. Sheila was cooking dinner, so I hopped up on the counter and just asked her how her day was."

"Yeah," said Sheila. "And then before I knew it, he was helping me set the table and cooking one of the dishes."

I have no idea what prompted Chad to make this overture, since he had absolutely no interest in doing it the previous week, but it was just what they needed. And because they were willing to keep doing this sort of thing, they began to have some "money in the bank" to start chipping away at their other issues. There just isn't any way we could have gotten there if they had been unwilling to participate in the positive side of the equation.

So, when it comes to the setup, the first thing is to decide if you really need to have a conflict. Maybe what you really need instead is a few deposits in your relationship bank. I know that things might be tense, but sometimes when annoyed, if you can set that issue aside for a bit and instead bank some deposits, you'll be in a better position to assess what really needs fixing. If you can't think of how to build positives, don't worry! That's what chapter 9 is all about.

Get an Attitude Adjustment

Okay, so say you have some positives in the bank, and there's still something going on that needs to be addressed. The next part of the setup for good conflict is to have a little talk with yourself and make sure you are coming at the conversation from the right place mentally. The dos and don'ts we talked about in chapter 3 are a part of this, but certain attitudes are also helpful to cultivate before you begin the fight.

The Don't-Know Mind

In Eastern philosophies, like Buddhism, there's a concept called the *don't-know mind*. It's just what it sounds like: having a stance that you just don't know everything. And it's very helpful during a conflict. Have you ever been wondering about something, and someone says, "You should ask your partner," and you say, "Oh, I already know what they'll say"? It's a common thought because when we know someone pretty well, we can often predict what they will think or how they will feel about a topic. But we don't really know, and this especially comes into play in conflict.

Given how our brain works, our memory of events can be affected by emotional experiences, so it's possible that we don't know our partner's intentions or why something happened the way it did. In fact, if we truly love each other and yet we've hurt each other, it's pretty much guaranteed that we don't know all the details of what happened! Unless your partner hurting you was intentional (which is an entirely different topic), then likely there are details you are unaware of about the conflict.

If you enter into the conflict assuming that there are a lot of things you don't know, then you're in a much better position to be curious and to listen to what your partner says when they're talking from their perspective.

Chad had a struggle to develop the don't-know mind. Very often he would gaze into that crystal ball, and he would say something like this:

> "She hates my family. My mom was rude to her once, and now Sheila is never going to let her back in."
>
> I turn to Sheila. "Is Chad correct about how you feel, Sheila?"
>
> "Not really," she says. "It's true that his mom and I had an altercation early on when we were planning our wedding. It was my wedding, and she really wanted to run the show. But there are actually a lot of things I really like about Ruth. I do want to establish some boundaries, though."
>
> "She wants my parents to stay in a hotel every time they visit!" shouts Chad.
>
> "Is that the case, Sheila?" I ask.
>
> "No, not at all. He doesn't get it," she says.

You can see how some kinds of assumptions can be deadly in an argument. So, before you begin, try to be aware of any assumptions you have about what your partner did, what they want, or what happened. If you do this, you'll be in a much better position to ask good questions and be curious—even if you're reading this book alone and your partner isn't participating. People love to talk about themselves, and most people respond really well to curiosity.

Us Against the Problem

Before you set up an argument, it's important to have an attitude of collaboration (I talked about this in chapter 2). The nature of an argument is that you feel one way and your partner feels another, so in essence it's "me against you." But this attitude isn't going to help you come up with a good discussion or resolution. The more you can square your mind into an "us against the problem" viewpoint, the better off you will be. Initially, Chad and Sheila felt it was "me against you." Chad wanted to have a relaxed, no-rules type of approach with his parents, and Sheila wanted to institute some boundaries to make their visits more acceptable to her. Chad versus Sheila.

But once they got to a place where their attitude was "Hey, we have a problem concerning Chad's parents, and we need to work together to come up with a solution," things were much easier to discuss. Sheila wasn't against Chad or his parents. She just needed to have some things in place to make their visits more comfortable for her. Chad wasn't against Sheila feeling comfortable—he loved her! He just needed to know that she supported his relationship with his parents.

I can't think of an argument that I've arbitrated between a couple that couldn't be shifted into an attitude of cooperation. If you truly love each other and are trying to make your lives work together better, then you need to find a way to work together and not against each other. And this begins with your attitude.

Again, if you're reading this book alone, you may think that you can't get your partner to shift into an "us against the problem" attitude. However, with individual clients who are working on their relationships, I suggest they use "we," "us," and "let's" language with their partners. This simple shift is profound; it sounds much less blaming when you say, "We should think about how we could handle this" than when you say, "I don't like how you handled this." Over time, your language will sound more like an invitation than a complaint, and I bet your partner will respond positively.

Being Open to Their Perspective

One of the things that crops up a lot in arguments is interpreting things from our own perspective. Of course, our perspectives—which are based on our own personalities and life experiences—are the only ones we have at our disposal because we're who we are! But a very important attitude to take, both in arguments with your partner and indeed in the world in general, is that the meaning of what someone else does is not necessarily the same as it would be if you did it.

Let me give you an example. When I was a kid, birthdays were a big deal. It wasn't just a birthday. It was more like birthday week! Birthday month, if I could get away with it! Also, gifts are my love language, so I really put a lot of stock in how I'm treated on my birthday. My husband, like I said, is the youngest of fourteen children, so his family was different. His family was more like, "Oh, it's your birthday. Here's five dollars. Go buy yourself a cake." (It wasn't quite that bad, but you get the point.) I'm sure you see the disaster coming. Yep, the first year we were dating, my husband showed up at my work with lit cupcakes in front of all my coworkers. So sweet! I was thrilled. But…that was it. That was all that happened. No other surprises, no gifts, nothing.

To him, though, showing up at work with lit cupcakes was an acknowledgment of my birthday, a surprise, and a thoughtful gesture—and it was! To appreciate the gesture for what it was, I had to be able to see where he was coming from.

You can see how the tendency to be stuck in your own perspective can get you into trouble in myriad ways. Yet it's all too common.

Returning to the previous example, Chad believed that setting boundaries and putting restrictions on someone's behavior must mean you are upset with them or that you don't like them. That perspective came from his own family experience, and he assumed that when Sheila wanted to establish boundaries with his mom, she must be upset with his mom or just not like her. In reality, Sheila was an only child in a family that had very clear boundaries and distinctions, and she had a hard time tolerating the "chaos" of Chad's family sometimes, so she simply wanted to put some rules around behaviors that would help her be more comfortable.

I'm constantly asking couples "Is that true?" or "Are they right about what you're thinking?" and so on, because the partners are not asking those questions and making the necessary distinctions between what they think and what their partners think. And if you want to have healthy conflicts, you need to get this straight in your mind before you start. The other person is not you. The things they say and do are not motivated by the same thoughts and feelings you have.

In the Druid Vow of Friendship, there's the line "I hold no cherished outcome." Most of us go into a conflict definitely holding on to the outcome we want. We absolutely know how we want this to go and how we want it to end. But if—and I know it's a big if—you can adhere to this vow, to hold no cherished outcome, things will likely turn out better. After all, there may be outcomes you haven't even dreamed of; there might be options you haven't even thought of! So be open to what might happen and hold loosely to your own opinion about what the best outcome might be.

Principles of the Setup

So now you've decided that you need to have a conflict, you have "money" in your relationship bank, and you have the right attitudes. The next step is to have a conflict conversation when you're *not* already mad.

When I talk to couples about this, they sometimes say, "Why would I want to have a conflict conversation when I'm not already mad? Why would I ruin a perfectly good Saturday morning with an argument when everything is going well?" By now, however, you know enough to understand the importance of timing your conflict conversations. Otherwise, explosive conflict may derail your relationship, and there will be no more peaceful Saturday mornings together.

For Chad and Sheila, the only time they ever discussed Chad's family was when something triggered their conversation, and it usually wouldn't go well. Sheila might overhear Chad on the phone talking to his parents about coming up to visit for a week or about them all going on vacation together, and she'd just blow her top. She was triggered, and probably in fight-or-flight mode, so the way she would begin the argument was typically not very productive. And because it was accusatory, Chad would immediately drop into fight-or-flight mode too.

"You are such a jerk!" she'd yell. "I can't believe after all this time you're just inviting your family without even talking to me!"

Chad was actually planning to talk to her about it, but he sure wouldn't admit it after that.

"They're my family. How dare you try to dictate when I can and can't see my family!" he would yell back. And they were off to the races.

Now, I've rarely met a couple who doesn't know what their differences are when I ask them in the calm environment of my office. When I asked Chad and Sheila what their issues were and what they argued about, they both immediately knew: finances and Chad's family. So, it's not like they didn't know where their differences lay. They did know. They just avoided the topic unless it came up, because every time it did come up, there was a ridiculously painful argument.

Of course, even after you're adept at healthy conflict, some arguments will continue to simply pop up out of nowhere. Let's say you're driving and your partner complains that you're taking a roundabout route or something, and an argument erupts. Sometimes that's just what's going to happen. But the dynamics of this conversation might be ones you'd be able to anticipate. Maybe you're sensitive about being controlled in situations like these, or maybe your partner is on the controlling side. This would probably have shown up in a multitude of ways and situations before this moment. So, the *theme* of your argument isn't sudden or surprising. You could absolutely schedule a calm conversation to talk about your partner's controlling ways or your unreasonable sensitivities.

In fact, the only time you ever have to address a conflict the moment it flares up is when it is absolutely urgent, and there's a difference of opinion. I'm going to address this situation in chapter 10 when answering some common questions and troubleshooting. For now, I'll just ask you to consider how many of your common spontaneous conflicts have a theme that could be addressed when you're not in conflict. As another example, say you and your partner are at your child's school learning about sports, and today is the last day to sign up. You want to do it, your spouse doesn't, and the decision has to be made now. Clearly this can't wait. But the theme is probably not new. If it's a money issue (difference of opinion on how much you should be spending on your kid's extracurricular activities) or a time issue (different ideas on how many activities little Johnny should do), this is not the first time the issue has come up. And while, yes, this particular issue must be decided now, the larger issue can be addressed in a scheduled, structured conflict conversation.

Setting Up the Conflict Conversation

Let's take a look at what a good setup looks like, when all the advice we've explored so far is put into play. Say Sheila hears Chad on the phone talking with his family about coming for a visit. She notices that this is a trigger and that it's making her really mad. She also knows that it's imperative not to talk when you are already mad, so she just observes and accepts her emotions. Because she knows her body and understands her physiology, she can feel that she has crossed over into some level of fight or flight. She takes some deep, mindful breaths and reminds herself that they can have a conversation about the phone call at a better time. Then she walks past Chad in her running clothes and says, "Hey, I'm going for a quick jog!", which is her preferred committed calming activity.

Setting the Appointment

Sheila returns from her run feeling better. She asks Chad what he wants to do for dinner, and they set about making it. As they work, Sheila reminds herself of a few things. First, she knows Chad loves her and wouldn't want to make her uncomfortable; she gives him the benefit of the doubt. She reminds herself that she does not know what Chad's intentions were, and also that she could hear only one side of the conversation, so she really doesn't have all of the information. Finally, she reminds herself that this isn't her way against Chad's way. Dealing with Chad's boisterous family is something that the two of them will have to work on together, maybe for a long time. With this in mind, she takes the next step:

"Hey, Chad, earlier I overheard you talking with your family about coming to visit. Do you think we could sit down and talk about how we can make it a good visit for both of us? I love that you are such a family person, but I also want to talk about some of the things that I need to feel comfortable while they're here. When would be a good time for you to talk?"

Sheila's method contains all of the good elements of setting up a conflict conversation. First, she states what happened that she noticed or that was a problem for her, and she does it not in an accusatory or angry way. She then voices her request and her appreciation of her partner. Last, she lets him know more specifically what she wants to talk about, and she lets him have control over when that conversation will take place.

In response, Chad feels himself getting immediately defensive, but he's committed not to behave that way; he's successfully changed his mindset on this. He knows his family is a problem for Sheila, and he knew she was within earshot when he was having the conversation, so he was prepared for war when he hung up the phone. But now he's getting a compliment and a clear, polite request for discussion. He knows what the topic is, he has control over when the conversation will happen, and he has time to think about what he would like to say.

"How about if we eat dinner and then we can sit out on the back porch and talk about it?" he offers. Sheila gladly accepts.

Do you see how this is so much better than if Sheila had just popped off as soon as Chad hung up the phone? Neither of them now has dysregulated physiology, they have a collaborative attitude, and the conversation is set up to succeed. This is a beautiful setup, and we'll catch up with these two in the next chapter!

But first, consider what might have happened if Sheila had been reading this book on her own (without Chad) and she had used these same setup techniques when Chad got off the phone. Chad would have been expecting her to get irate. Wouldn't he have been surprised if she just went for a jog and then came back and invited him into a conversation with this setup? I bet he would, and I bet he would accept her invitation. Or what if it was Chad who had been reading this book? Sheila might have started yelling at him as soon as he got off the phone, but Chad would have stayed calm because he'd been practicing calming techniques. (Note that he might not feel calm, but Chad no longer behaves according to his feelings.) Then Chad would have invited Sheila to have a conversation a little later. Sheila might not have taken him up on it because she was used to duking it out in the moment. But even if the only difference was that Chad stayed calmer, it would have been a great start. He might have circled back around later to set up a calmer conversation. Let's see how you might practice some of this.

EXERCISE: Identifying Topics and Themes

You know what your issues with your partner are, right? If you're like Chad and Sheila, your issues would be family and finances. And when family or finances come up as topics of conflict, there are probably some underlying themes, like control versus sensitivity. List the topics of most of your arguments, and try to group them into themes. If you're reading this book with your partner, you may want to do this exercise separately and then compare what you have done to see if you're on the same page.

If your partner is not participating, you can still do this exercise. Hopefully you'll be able to think of all the different topics that you argue about. Try thinking of things that your partner would list—maybe they are topics you care less about!

If this exercise is difficult to do because you're having a hard time defining your issues and themes, chapter 8 covers some common ones for couples, which may help you define yours.

EXERCISE: Starting the Process of Change

Looking at your list of topics, rank them from the most to the least serious. Then choose one of the least serious to practice with. For example, if your topics are sexual issues, financial disparities, and vacation preferences, I'd choose vacation preferences to start practicing on. If you're doing this exercise with your partner, combine your two lists of conflict topics and then rank them.

Now have a short setup conversation about the issue you want to discuss. If you're reading this book with your partner, whoever is usually triggered should begin. First state the issue that you have, see if you can find something authentic that you can appreciate about your partner when it comes to this issue, and then ask your partner when a good time would be to discuss this. The other person then chooses a time when the two of you can have a productive conversation. Whoever makes this choice should resist the urge to say "six months from now!" If possible, it's good to schedule the conversation for some time in the next couple of days.

If you're doing this exercise on your own, I suggest waiting until your least serious conflict topic comes up—the next time you're talking about vacations, for example. Try modeling your response on the suggestions in this chapter. If your partner isn't very receptive to a conversation, they might suggest a time weeks from now. That's okay! Just back off for now and try again later. Hopefully with gentle encouragement, they'll be willing to try.

Moving Forward

How did your setup conversation go? If you were able to put the suggestions into practice to good effect, great! If it was a little rockier than you hoped it would be, that's fine too. Patience and persistence are key. Remember to also consistently practice your calming activities so you can easily access them when you need to.

It's finally time to have your actual conflict conversations, and the next two chapters are going to walk you through exactly how to do them!

CHAPTER 6

Conflict Conversation Number 1

This chapter introduces what's known as the speaker–listener method of communication, which is an essential piece of your road map for conflict. This way of communicating will help you and your partner hear and understand each other before you move into finding solutions for your conflicts. I have clients who initially resist this method because it doesn't feel "authentic" or natural, and I agree! But my question to them is, "How is your authentic communication going for you"? Clearly not well.

I'm all for being authentic, but there are times when it's actually overrated, and this is one of those times. In fact, we're often not fully authentic, because we realize it would be inappropriate. For example, if your boss is being a jerk, you don't tell her she's being a jerk, do you? If your kids are driving you crazy and you're having one of those days when you wish you could hide, you don't say, "I wish I could hide from you," because you know that would be unhelpful. Likewise, authentic communication in an argument off-loads everything that's in your mind, and when you're trying to solve a problem, this isn't going to get you anywhere. So you may have to shift your attitude into accepting that you will be practicing something that is clunky and awkward at first, but it will feel more natural the more you do it.

Listening, Understanding, and Validating

Conflict conversation number 1 is all about listening, understanding, and validating. This first conversation is meant solely to gain understanding. Most of us move way too quickly toward seeking solutions, and the problem with that is that we don't fully understand each other yet. People who feel misunderstood resist most suggestions, which means that speeding past the understanding part doesn't contribute to healthy conflict. It's mightily tempting to move on to solutions, though, so you can visit http://www.newharbinger.com/51697 to print out some cards to remind yourself that you're in conversation number 1: listening, and not conversation number 2: solutions, or you can make your own.

Ideally, you've set an appointment for this conversation, you know what the topic to be discussed is, and you are managing your physiological responses. That's where Chad and Sheila are when they sit down after dinner to discuss his family. Chad and Sheila's conversation follows the speaker–listener method of listening, understanding, and validating. First I'll break down the conversation into the steps they will follow.

Step 1: Speaker A Speaks

Sheila is the one who is upset and has a problem in this situation, so she should begin the conversation. She is Speaker A. Speaker A has a set amount of time to speak about the situation. What is it that is upsetting to them? How do they feel about it? What are their thoughts about it? If Speaker A is a verbal processor who talks a lot, it's helpful to break this up into smaller chunks. In this case, Sheila just starts with what is upsetting to her.

Step 2: Speaker B Repeats It Back

Speaker B—Chad—now repeats back his understanding of what Speaker A said. Speaker B likely has a lot of feelings about what Speaker A has said—and maybe even some choice words—but it's not time for Speaker B's feelings. Step 2 is solely for Speaker B to repeat back what they heard.

Now, it may feel weird to say, "So, what I heard you say is..." and then use the exact same words the other person just used. But every single time I have done this with clients, they feel very heard, and when I can get my clients to do it with each other, I receive the same positive report. It turns out that when someone repeats back to you what they heard you say, in your words, to see if they really understood, it feels really, really good.

After Speaker B repeats back what they heard Speaker A say, Speaker B asks, "Did I get that right?" Note that it is imperative that Speaker B's tone be as respectful as possible, and at the very least neutral. It's important to steer clear of disrespectful body language, such as eye rolling.

Step 3: Speaker A Corrects, If Necessary

Let's say that Speaker B did a pretty good job repeating back what they heard, but they missed a detail or got a detail wrong. This step gives Speaker A an opportunity to clarify what they meant and restate their thought. Once again, Speaker B repeats back what they heard and asks, "Do I have it right now?"

Step 4: Empathize and Validate, If Possible

Once Speaker B has repeated back correctly, they can take a moment to really imagine how they would feel if what Speaker A said were true. If they felt exactly how Speaker A feels, can they understand how Speaker A is feeling?

A word about empathy, which is what you're using here: empathy is not the same as agreeing. That is, you can express empathy even if you vehemently disagree with what Speaker A is saying or feel that their viewpoint is utterly skewed. You can say, "I can understand what you are saying. If I felt that's what happened, I would be upset as well." That's an empathic response. Note that you're not agreeing that this is what happened. You're just saying that if you believed that's what happened, you'd be upset too. Or you can validate something the other person has just said. For example, "I hear what you are saying, and I completely agree that my mom can be overwhelming" would really go a long way.

However, a word of caution: empathy or validation must be authentic. Don't say you can understand it unless you do. Don't validate something that you feel is really untrue. Only make this statement if you can find something that you do understand or do agree with, and there is usually something, even if it's something very small.

At this point, if you've been breaking down Speaker A's many thoughts and feelings into smaller chunks, you go back and do steps 1 through 4 as many times as necessary until Speaker A feels completely heard and understood on the issue in question.

Steps 5 through 8: Reverse Speakers

Now you switch places and go back through the entire sequence, with Speaker B talking about their experiences, thoughts, and feelings. Speaker A repeats back and asks if they have gotten it right until they have accurately repeated back what Speaker B has said. Speaker A then can empathize with or validate anything possible.

Optional Step 9: Reviewing the Conversation

Lastly, you can review the conversation to look for areas where the two of you may feel the same way. Sometimes this is helpful. Having gone into a conflict conversation feeling like you are worlds apart, it can be a relief to recognize ways you actually do agree with each other, either in the details of what happened or in how you feel or think about it. After this, you can also make a list of the places where you do not have a meeting of the minds or where you feel differently. Again, it's optional, but it can sometimes provide a good guide for the second conflict conversation about solutions to the issue, which will be covered in the next chapter.

All of these steps are generally easy to grasp when you see them written out, but actually putting them into practice can be more difficult. For example, the speaker might be talking about the issue, and you are supposed to be the listener, listening to repeat back, but instead you get caught up in how you feel or all the ways you want to make a rebuttal to their story. A therapist friend of mine came up with the idea of red and yellow laminated cards, labeled "speaker" and "listener," for the parties to hold as reminders to themselves which role they are currently occupying. You can also have an object that the speaker holds to remind both of you that it's their turn right now to do the talking. You can visit http://www.newharbinger.com/51697 to download a set of speaker and listener cards, or you can create your own.

Chad and Sheila's Conversation

Here's what Chad and Sheila's conversation looks like when they conduct their conversation using the speaker–listener method.

Step 1: Sheila Speaks

Again, because Sheila is the one who wants to talk, she begins. Chad understands that she has the floor and that his role is only listening for the time being. Because Chad knows that he's likely to be triggered by what Sheila says, he is consciously taking deep breaths to keep himself calm.

Sheila: "Okay, so I want to talk about how I feel about your family. Obviously, you know that I was an only child, and my parents honestly just treated me mostly like a little adult. When we initially got together, I loved your huge, chaotic family because it was something that I never had. But when we were planning our wedding, I learned the other side of the coin. Your mom was always telling me what I needed to do, like I couldn't possibly do it myself. And there are still times now when she tells me how to parent, and it really triggers something ugly in me. I know she's just trying to be helpful, but it's hard for me to have someone butt in with their opinions without even asking. I have more to say, but maybe we should make sure you understand at least this part before we go on."

Sheila has several other things that she wants to address, so she's going to take the process in smaller chunks. Now it's time for Chad to summarize what he heard Sheila say.

Step 2: Chad Repeats Back

Chad begins by pausing and taking a deep breath to remain calm. Then he says, "All right, what I heard you say is that you were an only child and left largely on your own growing up. At first you liked my family because it was different, but then when it came to planning our wedding, things switched around a bit. You don't like it when my mom tells you what to do—back then with the wedding and now with the kids. You think she is overwhelming. Did I get that right?"

As the reader, you can pause for a second and ask yourself if you think Chad got that right, and if not, what is his misunderstanding?

Step 3: Sheila Corrects Chad

Sheila feels herself internally being triggered by Chad telling her that she thinks his mom is overwhelming. First of all, that's not what she said, and second, she's really triggered when people assume how she is feeling or what she is thinking with a *you-statement*. Normally in an argument, this is where Sheila would start yelling something like, "Don't tell me how I feel!" and things would start to spiral downward. But now, she pauses to settle herself a bit and then takes the opportunity given to correct Chad's assumption.

"Actually, that's not quite right," says Sheila. "You got most of it right, but not that last sentence. I don't necessarily think your mom is overwhelming. I think she's trying to be helpful. I don't dislike her, and I'm not attributing bad motives to her. I get overwhelmed when she starts telling me what to do, but I don't think she is trying to be overwhelming, if that makes sense."

Step 4: Chad Empathizes and Validates

Chad takes Sheila's correction and responds: "Okay, thanks for helping me understand that distinction. I can see the difference. I hear what you're saying about your experiences with my family. I don't like when my boss comes across as telling me what to do when I already know what I'm doing, so I can understand your feeling like that and not liking it."

At this point, Sheila is feeling heard and understood about this first part and feels that Chad is on her side. During the next part of the conversation, Sheila and Chad go back to step 1 and repeat the process through step 4, talking about each of Sheila's other concerns in turn: how long the family visits are, the fact that there are no boundaries to these visits, and Sheila's ideas about what to do about it. They repeat these steps until Sheila feels like she has said all that she wants to say on the topic and feels that Chad understands.

As it is a long process, Sheila and Chad decide to take a short break before switching sides to give room for Chad to be heard. (Honestly, it's easier if you do this process with only one topic, or even a part of one topic, to make it less exhausting. And it's better to have these conversations more often about smaller topics than to try to solve something huge all in one go.)

For the purpose of illustrating how these conversations work, I want to switch sides now to show Chad's turn at saying how he feels. Until now, Sheila was holding a speaker card, and Chad the listener card, to remind them both of the roles they're occupying in the conversation. They switch cards now so that it's clear that Chad is the speaker. They also smile at each other, take a deep breath, and get ready for a change in the conversation.

Step 5: Chad Speaks

Chad has been frustrated for some time by the relationship between Sheila and his mom, so he has quite a bit to say. He knows that he has a tendency to get fired up about it, and he's pretty determined to stay calm, but he also knows that he and Sheila have a time-out agreement if he needs it, so he begins:

"Well, obviously I grew up in this family, so this kind of chaos and opinionated discourse is just the norm for me. I probably fell in love with you because you're the opposite, so calm. But it was really hard for me when we were planning our wedding. Yeah, I know Mom had strong opinions about what we should and shouldn't do, but I would have told her just to go pound dirt! I felt like you actually were the one who escalated things by the way you responded. It was like you would get super mad at what she was saying, but you didn't tell her—she had no idea! Instead, you came and complained to me (and really anyone else who would listen), and I felt like that just made you madder and madder instead of solving anything! And then my mom was totally in the dark. She didn't even know you were mad! I think this happens a lot, where things could be resolved at the lowest level if you would just speak up right away and say you don't like something."

Step 6: Sheila Repeats Back

Now it's Sheila's turn to reflect back what Chad is saying. Unfortunately, Sheila's not doing a good job at listening without reacting, so she tries but gets derailed by her emotions.

"So, what I hear you saying is that it's all my fault. I'm the problem. Your precious mom is just being herself and trying to help, and I'm the one who is always causing the problems. Honestly, why are we even doing this? You're never going to really understand my side of things!"

Sheila's statement is an example of a faulty mental filter (see chapter 2). She paid attention to only one part of what Chad was saying. Chad can't help piping in, "I listened to you when you were talking! Why can't you stay on task? This is exactly what I'm talking about! Yeah, you're the problem!"

Oh boy. They're both really worked up now. However, Sheila is able to see that she's gotten them off track. She's still really upset and she really, really wants to fire back in kind. But they've been practicing this for a while, and Sheila knows that continuing this talk isn't going to be helpful now that they're both upset, so she calls a time-out with a hand signal they've agreed upon. There's a beat where Chad looks at her unbelievingly, and she's afraid it's not going to work, but then his shoulders drop and he walks away. His walking away used to be a huge trigger for Sheila, but it isn't now. They've previously agreed on the process for time-outs: she knows it will last for thirty minutes, and then they will try again. There isn't time for a jog, so Sheila decides to walk around the block. While she walks, Sheila practices mindfulness and tries to notice what she is seeing, smelling, and hearing and tries not to think back on the conversation or the things Chad said that got her so worked up.

Thirty minutes later, they're back in the same spot and ready to try again.

Step 6, Again: Sheila Repeats Back

Sheila begins: "Okay, Chad, let's try this again, and I'm going to try to get it right this time. You really liked how calm I was when we first met. But it was hard for you when I became upset with your mom during the wedding planning. You feel like you would have just told her what's what, but you think that I talked to everyone but her. Did I get that right?"

Sheila has now done a pretty good job of reflecting back Chad's thoughts. She stepped out of being offended about what he was saying and is able to just repeat back what she heard. This isn't the time to agree or disagree or to move into what to do about it. It's the time to really try to understand, so that's what Sheila is doing now.

Step 7: Chad Corrects, If Necessary

Because Sheila did a pretty good job of reflecting back what Chad said, there isn't much to say here. Chad tells her she did a good job, and then he adds that he isn't saying it's her fault; this is just how he feels.

Step 8: Sheila Empathizes and Validates

Sheila is pretty calm now, and she thinks about how it might feel if someone ranted to her about something but refused to talk to the person they were actually upset with. She's had this experience before, where a friend always wanted to vent to her but was unwilling to go to the person they were mad at, and she didn't like it. So she's able to understand how Chad was feeling.

"Wow, okay, yeah I know I don't like it when people complain to me but aren't willing to try to fix the problem," she begins. "I can see how it must have felt for you to have to hear me complain about your mom all that time when I was not really willing to talk to her about it. I would've been annoyed too."

Chad nods. This is just one part of the issue that they are discussing, so their actual conversation goes on much longer. But you can see how at this point they are both feeling pretty heard and understood by the other person. The process hasn't been perfect, but the time-out was really effective at getting them back on track.

Step 9: Coming Together

Again, step 9 is optional. In this step, the two of you look for ways you feel the same and ways you feel differently about the topic you are discussing. Here's how it goes when Chad and Sheila try doing it for the part of the conversation they've had thus far.

Chad begins: "Okay, let's see if we can figure out where we feel the same and where we feel differently. I think we both agree that my mom is just trying to be helpful. We both understand that it's hard for you to be told what to do. But I think we feel differently on how to solve that part! Is that what you think too?"

Sheila responds: "Yeah, I agree your mom is trying to be helpful, and I'm not very good at accepting that. I think you don't realize how upset I feel when it's happening, so I think you want me to say something in the moment, and I'm not sure I can do that. So in our second conversation, we'll have to figure out what is the best way to handle that."

This is great because now both of them agree that his mom is coming from a good place and trying to be helpful. This is going to be useful when it comes to solving the problem, because it'll drive how they decide to respond. If they thought she was coming from a malicious place, the solution would be different. (This first conversation does not always reveal similar feelings; sometimes it's the opposite and you realize how far apart you are. That's okay. Remember that this conversation is just to understand each other's feelings, not to come up with solutions.) They still disagree on whether or not Sheila should say something, but that's a topic now shelved for the solution conversation (see chapter 7).

I'm sure you can see that this isn't an easy process. Focused listening doesn't come naturally, and it takes practice. It is also very tempting to start talking about what to do about the issue. But that part doesn't belong in this first conversation. For now, Chad and Sheila call it a day and just enjoy the fact that they have had a productive conversation and both feel heard and understood. Before moving on to other things, Sheila asks when Chad would like to schedule their second conversation, and they decide that they'll have time to talk about it on the weekend. Off they go to make some emotional deposits while they're waiting for the opportunity for their next conversation.

A Word About Boundaries

It's important in discussions like these to be very clear on where you end and someone else begins. It's easy to get triggered if you aren't clear on what belongs to whom. For example, Chad might get triggered by what Sheila said if he felt like it was his job to "save" her from his chaotic family. Sheila does get triggered when she feels Chad is saying that all of this is her fault; that it has nothing to do with him. She may have interpreted that as him saying she's on her own and he's going to do nothing to help her. Now, Chad might indeed feel like Sheila has some responsibility in these interactions with his mom, and he also might feel like Sheila could do a lot of things differently. This isn't Sheila's problem! It is simply Chad's opinion. They actually don't have to feel the same on this issue to understand each other or solve the issue. But in conflicts, we often get caught up in the fact that someone feels very differently than we do, and we have trouble just detaching and being able to listen and see things from their perspective.

There are entire books on boundaries, and if you feel that you have trouble in this area, working on it will improve all of your relationships. Boundary work in general is beyond the scope of this book. However, I will repeat the little trick I mentioned in chapter 3. A good way not to be triggered in these conversations is to pretend, if only temporarily, like your partner is talking about someone else. You can step back into the conversation when it is your turn to talk about your feelings, but it's not time for that when you're listening. If you can pretend that this is a good friend of yours, talking about someone else they are upset with—that it's nothing personal—it will free you up to really listen to what they're saying, and to retain it, so that you can repeat it back. If you can put yourself in their shoes, it will be easier to validate or empathize with something that they have said.

How to Do This on Your Own

On an entirely different note, you can conduct conversation number 1 even if your partner is not reading this book with you or is not on board with this process. Typically, when having this conversation, the person who's upset is the first person to speak. But if you're doing this on your own, and you're the one who is upset, it's unlikely that your partner will invite you to talk about how you feel. If that were happening already, you wouldn't be reading this book!

My suggestion is to try to go through this process with your partner (unknowingly) being Speaker A. In other words, you've probably done a version of the setup from the previous chapter, and now it's time to have conversation number 1. You might say something like, "I'd really like to hear all about your perspective about what happened yesterday," inviting them to be the first speaker and just tell you their story or their feelings. Then you can say something like, "I'd really love to kind of reflect back to you what you're saying to make sure I understand it correctly. Would that be okay?" Most people are not going to refuse the opportunity to be heard and understood. Be sure to ask if you got it right and then validate or empathize if you can.

Afterward, you can't expect your partner to say, "Now it's your turn!" They're not reading this book, and they probably don't understand the process. If they do say, "Well, what about you?" that's great! Take them up on it. But otherwise, I would just leave the conversation where it is. Understanding your partner's point of view can be enough for now. You're playing the long game, betting on the odds that at some future point, feeling understood in a calm, loving way is going to be so compelling, they will want to return the favor. This might take some time. Don't expect the steps to be as systematic as presented in this chapter, and don't expect reciprocation right away. By doing something different, you are really trying to win over your partner. Believe in this process and just keep doing the best you can. I have seen relationships completely turn around when only one person is making this effort.

Okay, now that you've gotten all the tools you'll need, it's time to practice!

EXERCISE: Conducting Conversation 1

You've figured out what your issues are and set an appointment to have a conversation about one of them. Now, as you prepare to have this first conversation, it might be helpful to have the steps of the process written out in front of you, to know what your time-out signal is, if you have one, and to get into the right mindset to speak and repeat whatever you hear nonjudgmentally. Figure out who will be the first speaker, and off you go! Remember not to start with your biggest issue, and to break down your larger issues (as Chad and Sheila did) so that you can successfully discuss one small aspect of the problem.

Don't expect this to go perfectly the first time. This is just practice. You don't have to be perfect! If you've been having ineffective arguments for some time, it may take a while before this new system feels normal or begins to work smoothly. Also, do not expect to feel thoroughly satisfied after this first conversation, because it is not meant to actually resolve anything. We are so used to moving straight into resolution that stopping after we've understood each other can make the conversation feel incomplete. But it's important to keep practicing speaking and listening before you get into problem-solving mode.

Moving Forward

Everything in this book builds as you go, so remember to keep nurturing the conflict attitudes I've talked about and to practice the rules you've put in place and the calming techniques you've chosen. In the next chapter, you will (finally!) begin working on solutions. So put on your creativity hat and get ready to start brainstorming a multitude of new ideas.

CHAPTER 7

Conflict Conversation Number 2

Finally, after all of this prep work, we're ready to talk about problem-solving. If you've followed the process so far, you're likely eager to get started. Conflict conversation number 2 is the solution part of your conflict road map. Again, I'll walk you through the process of brainstorming and problem-solving and then show you how the conversation goes between Chad and Sheila.

Having an attitude of curiosity continues to be very important. As a general rule, throughout this process, if you get stuck on any step or point, a question is a better fallback than a statement. For example, let's say you are having conversation number 1 with your partner and they say something you find offensive. Instead of saying "I can't believe you think that!" (which I hope you can see by now would not be helpful), you can ask a clarifying question like "Are you saying…?" Even if you pretty much know the answer to your question, asking it has the benefit of buying you a little time to take a breath or activate whatever calming solutions that you feel work best for you. So, although asking questions and having curiosity isn't one of the formal steps, per se, it's always a good idea to be curious rather than presume that you know what your partner means or intends. Remember, you're not a mind reader!

Curiosity is also important when it comes to problem-solving. As I've said, we tend to approach conflict tied to the one solution that we already want. When we talk about solutions, we typically make a lot of statements and ask very few questions. But to come up with a solution that works for both of you, it's important to brainstorm a number of different possibilities. So the first step of this second conversation is for each of you to come to the table with multiple options so you can brainstorm together. This is another reason for the time lapse between conversations 1 and 2.

EXERCISE: List Some Potential Solutions

By now you've had a conversation with your partner about a small issue that you have, and hopefully you both feel like you have achieved a certain amount of understanding of the other person's perspective. Now it's time for each of you to come up with a list of five to ten potential solutions or compromises that would help the situation. Try to think outside the box here. The purpose is to get the conversation going in different ways with the goal of expanding the possibilities. For example, if you're discussing the problem of who should do the laundry, your options could be:

1. I do the laundry all the time, and my partner does something else in exchange.
2. My partner does the laundry all the time, and I offer to do something else in exchange.
3. We alternate weeks doing the laundry.
4. We each do our own laundry.
5. We have our kids do the laundry as one of the chores.
6. We hire the neighbors' kid to do it.
7. We just buy new clothes every time we run out!

Clearly, that last solution is silly, but ridiculous suggestions may help you think outside the box.

If you're making this list on your own, and not with your partner, try brainstorming five to ten ideas, leaning heavily on solutions that are okay with you but are things that you think your partner could get behind.

Did you have a hard time coming to the table with multiple solutions? If so, you may want to take advantage of some alternative viewpoints. If laundry is the issue, you can ask your friends what they do about laundry. If it's a parenting issue, you can log on to some parenting forums to see how other people are handling it. You can read articles. Anything that will generate ideas is great.

Brainstorming and Problem-Solving

The steps for this second conversation are not as lengthy or as difficult as those in the speaker–listener conversation covered in chapter 6. Here are the main steps.

Step 1: Brainstorm Multiple Options and Solutions

After each of you has come up with five to ten potential solutions, you'll come to the table and take turns discussing each one. Even though you probably have an option that you prefer, in this step try to give each option equal time and attention—again, not because every option is even plausible but because you may uncover a new possibility from just talking at length about the pros and cons. For example, looking at the list from the exercise above, the two of you would discuss the first option, in which one of you has suggested, "I do the laundry all the time, and my partner does something else." You might discuss whether you are actually willing to do the laundry all the time. What would that be like for you? Is there a task that you feel is equal in terms of labor and time that your partner could do? Is your partner willing to do it? How does your partner feel about you taking on this task? Or looking at the third option on the list, "We alternate weeks doing the laundry," what would it be like to alternate weeks? Is there any kind of noticeable difference in workload from week to week? What if it's one person's week and they can't do it for some reason—what happens then? Would there be a particular laundry day, or could it just be done any time in the week? Are there rules you'd need to agree on about how the laundry gets done?

There are usually many questions to ask about how any given option would work, how each person feels about that option, and what the overall effects of choosing it would be. If new options arise while you are talking, simply add them to the list and continue to talk until you have fully covered each and every option you can think of.

Conversation number 2 most often goes wrong when the couple hasn't come up with enough options. When Jeff and Bill did this process, they came back into my office saying that it didn't work. When I asked to see the list of the options they had discussed, they each had only two options on their list: each had written down the one they really wanted and then added a fairly ridiculous one. Doing that only served to reinforce a power struggle between them and led to an unproductive discussion. So when I say that you need five to ten options, I mean at least five each—and the more options, the better.

Step 2: Narrow the List

Now that you've discussed all the options, you can try to narrow down the possibilities. I tell my clients that you each get one veto option. It's very satisfying, so I would suggest doing it! You take your partner's list and cross off the option that is simply unacceptable to you, and they will do the same with your list. You can then look over your lists and decide together whether or not there are any options that you both agree will not work for the situation. These usually end up being the more ridiculous options, but not always! After this process, you should be left with at least four or five good options that might work.

Step 3: Imagine Living with the Options

For each remaining option, imagine yourselves living with it. You can take a few minutes and tell a story about what choosing this option might mean. How do each of you imagine feeling? Do you see any potential problems or future resentments? What will be the best thing about this option? What will be the worst? You can actually take a couple of days to do this step, to fully consider each option, and then return to the conversation. Or you can do this step without taking a break. But do resist the urge to hurry through it. Clearly, you will not be able to foresee all the ways each option might affect you, but if you spend enough time on this, you will have a good sense of how these different options would work and feel.

Step 4: Choose an Option

After all of this discussion, there might be an option that makes the most sense to both of you. If so, you're done. However, it normally doesn't work that way. There are often at least a couple of options that could be a good fit. I suggest experimenting with each possibility, trying it out for a few weeks and then trying out the other option (or options). See how they work. This will give you more information about the benefits and challenges of each.

It's also important to go into this knowing that whatever you choose will likely not be perfect and might not last forever. For example, I'm a spender and my husband is a saver, and that's a perpetual problem for us. We've come up with lots of solutions over the years that we are currently not practicing. They weren't bad solutions or bad decisions at the time, but eventually either something changed or we had a new idea that we thought might work better. When this happens, we don't become enemies! Instead we say, "Oh look, here we are talking about this issue again!" We view it as "us against the problem," so we go through the process again, as partners and teammates, not as adversaries.

Chad and Sheila's Conversation

Again, conversation number 2 is not as complex as conversation number 1. Here's how it works for Chad and Sheila.

Step 1: Brainstorm Multiple Options and Solutions

Chad and Sheila have had conversation number 1, and now they're going to try to come up with some solutions to the issue with Chad's family. Here is Sheila's list of possible solutions:

1. Have Chad talk to his mom about her behavior.
2. Chad and Sheila talk to his mom together.
3. Write a letter outlining boundaries for Chad's family visits.
4. Not let Chad's family visit at all.
5. Have Chad go visit his family to maintain his relationship with them.

Here is Chad's list of possible solutions:

1. Have Sheila get some therapy about why his family visits trigger her so much.
2. Have Sheila talk to his mom about what is bothering her.
3. Make a plan for Sheila to be busy with other things when his parents come.
4. Limit parent visits to a certain number of days.
5. Have his parents stay in a hotel when they visit.

Chad and Sheila will now discuss each and every option, giving equal attention to each, even if the conversation gets tense sometimes because they are not really on the same page. When they talk about Sheila's first option, Chad gets a little upset:

"Why do I have to talk to my mom? You're the one with the problem! It has nothing to do with me!"

Chad's words are blaming, which could be triggering, but Sheila takes a deep breath and keeps her cool. Then she explains why she thinks this might be a good option:

"I agree that you're not the one with the problem. But you are her son, and I would feel a little like I'm out of line having that conversation with her. Plus, the two of you get along so well, I figure she would be able to hear you much better and be able to make changes."

"Would you be there while I'm talking to her?" Chad wants to know.

"I could be if you think it would be helpful, but I'd rather not," says Sheila.

After completing their discussion about this option, they go on to discuss Chad's first option.

Sheila is not very happy about it: "Seriously? You think the solution is for me to get therapy because there's something wrong with me? That is so insulting!"

"No, I don't mean, 'You should get therapy because you're the problem,'" clarifies Chad. "I just mean that you might get some tools for coping with such a loud and boisterous family!"

"But how will that change the interaction between your mom and me?" Sheila wants to know. "Even if I'm coping better, I feel like there are still going to be situations that crop up with your mom that need to be addressed. So even if I do get therapy for myself, I don't think that addresses the problem we're talking about here."

Chad and Sheila continue to do this first step until they have talked about each option and their feelings about it. Now they are ready for step 2.

Step 2: Narrow the Options

Chad and Sheila use the veto option, so Chad crosses out the option of not having his family visit at all, and Sheila crosses out the plan for her to be "busy" when they arrive, because she doesn't want to feel kicked out of her own home. Chad and Sheila both decide that Sheila getting therapy might be a good idea but is not applicable in this particular case. They also agree that Chad going to visit his parents instead of his parents ever visiting is a bad option, because they both want their kids to have the experience of Grandma and Grandpa coming to visit. So that leaves them with six good options still on the table. They end up agreeing on the option of "Chad and Sheila talk to his mom together" because they both feel that even if Chad does all the talking, it might be good for Sheila to be there in case his mom needs further clarification or has questions.

They combine the option of writing a letter about boundaries for visits with the possibility of having his parents stay in a hotel or limiting the length of their visits. Whether they end up talking with his parents or sending a letter, they agree that it would be good to first further flesh out the boundaries they want to set.

So now they have two great ideas: talking to his mom together and outlining boundaries either in person or in a letter.

Step 3: Imagine Living with the Options

Chad and Sheila now have a long conversation about how a discussion with Chad's mom might go: What would Chad say? How do they think his mom might respond to each part? Do either of them see any potential rifts that might occur as a result of this conversation?

They also discuss the idea of boundaries and what those boundaries might need to be. Chad and Sheila agree to do this process again, each bringing five to ten boundary ideas and going through each option in the same way, to agree on what will work best.

Step 4: Choose an Option

After Chad and Sheila have another conversation about boundary options, they know that they want to talk to his mom and they know which boundaries they want to put in place. They decide that his mom might do better knowing the topics and boundaries in advance, so they decide to send her an email, saying they'd love to talk next time she comes up, and they list some of the topics and boundaries they'd like to discuss. They invite her to respond with any ideas she has too.

Chad and Sheila discuss the fact that different issues might crop up with his family in the future, and that this one solution isn't an answer to every problem that may come up. But now they know that this process is one they can turn to, whether it's to tinker with this solution or to come up with new ones. They feel good about what they've accomplished.

While conversation number 1 can often be very difficult and hard, conversation number 2 is usually a lot of fun. If you're doing it right and coming up with a multitude of options, then you're going to be talking about some things you haven't even previously thought of! Most of the time when I've done this myself or had clients do it, the option that we end up with is not one of the two narrow options we began with! It's better because it has been fully explored in an open, curious conversation.

Doing This on Your Own

Again, things are a bit different if you're doing this without your partner on board. Depending on how it's going with conversation number 1, you may want to just keep practicing it until things get to a more cooperative place and not try to move on to conversation 2 just yet. That's fine. Every relationship is different, so you can customize this process to fit whatever is happening as you proceed.

But what if your partner was somewhat receptive to the first conversation? Maybe they didn't ask how *you* felt or attempt to repeat back what your feelings were. But you do have a better idea of what they were thinking and feeling in the original conflict. Perhaps you can use this new knowledge to brainstorm on your own. You already know what your solution would be, but I bet you can also predict what your partner's top solution would be. Can you think of three or four other possibilities for solutions that might work for your partner? As I suggested before, you could search online, talk to your friends, and so on, and see if you can come up with five or six possibilities.

Then say something to your partner like, "I really loved hearing more about how you were feeling during that situation the other day! It changed my perspective a little bit. I'm wondering if it might be fun to brainstorm some creative ways that we could resolve it. Would you be interested in maybe doing that? I have a few ideas." Remember that this is a completely new concept to your partner. They might say no, and if they do, you can just back off to give them time to allow this new idea to sink in. You can try again on another issue or at a different time.

Another thing that might happen is that your partner will start thinking of new possibilities. It's kind of like when someone says, "Don't think about pink elephants," and then you can't stop thinking about pink elephants! You've brought up the idea that there may be more than only two solutions, which might be intriguing for them. They may say yes, or they may initially say no and then circle back around with some ideas of their own.

You might have to lean a little more heavily toward giving your partner a solution that makes more sense for them than for you. Again, you're playing the long game. You want your partner to see first that you're doing something really different, and then that this process is going to really work for them. Once they see that it is a really satisfying way of resolving problems, they may start asking you about what you are doing and get more on board with the entire process.

If they do go along with you on this process, it's important to let them know that this is just an experiment. You don't expect to come up with a solution that will be perfect and last forever. Present your final solutions as something to try for a while so your partner knows that if this idea doesn't work, it's no big deal! You can always brainstorm again.

EXERCISE: Conducting Conversation 2

At the beginning of this chapter, you and your partner each came up with five to ten possible solutions to a problem you've been discussing. Now that you've read this chapter, each of you can list any other ideas that may have come up. Afterward, sit down with your partner and go through the options on your list using the four steps described in this chapter to see if you can come up with a solution that seems workable. Decide on a time period to experiment with this solution, and then sit down at the end of that time period and discuss how it has gone. Even if it's the solution you really love, be open to your partner saying it's not working for them. There are always more ideas!

You're now at the end of this conflict process. As with many new things, it's much easier to say and to read about than to actually put into practice. Learning something new, especially when emotions are running high, is hard. Be patient with yourself and understand that you are unlearning a long time (perhaps years!) of doing things differently. You'll need to practice this method many times before it seems natural. One thing to note is that when you get really good at this process, you can sometimes combine the two conversations. But until you feel like you are at an expert level, I'd keep them separate.

Moving Forward

While every couple has their own unique set of problems, I find that their issues often fall into these categories: household tasks, parenting, in-law relationships, money, and sex. Of course, you can resolve your challenges in these areas by simply following the process outlined in part 2. But there are also some tried-and-true ways to talk about and resolve these issues that may provide a good starting point. That will be the topic of the next chapter, which begins part 3.

PART 3

Resolving Your Differences

CHAPTER 8

Common Issues Between Couples

You should now feel like you have a good road map for conflict and be able to discuss your conflicts step-by-step. Although the conversations presented in part 2 can get you through whatever comes your way, it may also help to look at some common topics of conflict between couples. Let's face it. Most couples fight about the same five things: household tasks or workload fairness, money or finances, in-laws or family, parenting, and sex. There are some basics about each of these issues that I think would apply to almost any couple. This chapter is meant to give some guidance on each of these issues so that you're armed with some general knowledge about them before attempting to follow the conflict road map.

Household Tasks and Workload Fairness

Workload fairness in household tasks comes up so often with couples that it's surprising. But it makes sense, too, because none of us wants to feel taken advantage of or like we're pulling more weight than others. And since we all grew up in different families, learned different ways of handling this, and have different tolerances for neatness and cleanliness, this topic is bound to crop up in almost every relationship. For example, we have dogs, and I have to admit that I just don't see the dog hair on the wood floors like my husband does! And likewise, I feel the need to clean the tub and toilets a little more than he does. This kind of thing could—and does—derail relationships all the time. I confess that I sometimes say to myself, *Really? You're going to lose your marriage over toilet cleaning?* But of course, as I said, it's not really about the toilets, is it?

When Brenda and Sally came in, they were ready to quit. Sally was furious that she was always doing the cleaning, and all of her requests for help seemed to fall on deaf ears. Yes, it's true that Brenda worked full-time and Sally worked only part-time, but then Sally spent more time taking the kids all the places they needed and wanted to go—it wasn't like she was sitting around eating bonbons. I asked them the question I always ask, "So, at the beginning of your relationship, how did you negotiate who would do what?" and I got the same response I always get: deer in the headlights.

"Huh? We didn't! Do people do that?" asked Brenda.

No, actually most people don't—but they should. Most of us get together and fall in love living in separate spaces. Most of the time, things from one place just migrate into the other place, or we move in together and we continue to do what we're already used to doing. Even if people are pretty intentional about having shared duties, they generally don't sit down to sort out exactly who will do what. And of course, it's easy to see how this goes wrong: the cleaner person ends up doing more and resenting it mightily. If this has become an issue for you, then negotiating who will do what is an important process to undertake. While it might seem clunky or overly structured, I think you will find that being as intentional as possible in this negotiation helps conflict in this area quite a bit.

I suggest as part of your conflict conversation to sit down and mindfully decide what tasks will fall to whom, when they will do them, and how. If both people work full-time, the workload distribution at home should be pretty close to fifty-fifty. If, like Brenda and Sally, there is a disparity in time at work, the workload distribution at home can be shifted accordingly. It's also very important to understand that this agreement is being made based on how things are in the present and therefore will need to be adjusted if things change. If Brenda gets laid off or retires and Sally is still working part-time, Sally should not be asked to continue doing 70 percent of the tasks. Additionally, you may have to come to an agreement about whether a task needs to be done at all and about what exactly constitutes a task being done or completed.

A good place to start is to make a list of all your household tasks. I like to break these down into daily, weekly, monthly, and seasonal lists. Main categories might be cleaning, outside tasks, vehicle tasks, finances, pet duties, and child duties if you have children. You can visit http://www.newharbinger.com/51697 to download a sample list. Once you have a list of everything that you and your partner agree needs to be done, you'll be ready for the next steps I encourage my clients to take:

1. Decide together what the workload split should be, based on how much each of you works outside the home.

2. Sit down together with the list so that each of you can claim the items you like to do or don't mind doing. After this, check the split. So, for example, if Brenda and Sally have agreed to a sixty-forty split in duties, we want to make sure that Brenda has four items marked for every six that Sally has. Also, because there are daily tasks, weekly tasks, and monthly tasks, make sure that you achieve equality as closely as you can; in other words, if I pick a daily task and my partner picks a monthly task, those need to be equivalent in terms of the workload itself, or the total time we each put into doing this work on a monthly basis.

3. Sort out the items that neither of you wants or likes to do. First, decide if these items need to be done. Then, either make agreements ("Okay, I'll clean the toilets if you mow the lawn") or

decide if it makes sense to pay someone to do these tasks for you—an option you can take if it's available.

4. Finally, define what it looks like for these tasks to be finished properly. Sometimes what you think is a finished product is not the same as what your partner thinks. So it's useful to agree on what it looks like for each task to be completed.

As in any solution to conflict, these distributions of household work may not last forever; things will change, or you'll get tired of mowing the lawn and want to switch it out for something else. In that case, you can simply go back through the process to renegotiate the tasks.

Money and Finances

Most couples have differences when it comes to money, finances, and budget. And again, this makes sense because money carries a lot of meaning and all families conduct their financial lives differently. There is an underlying meaning to all things financial, and it's important to know what money means to your partner.

Bill and Jane get into trouble with finances every time. It's not only because Bill is a spender and Jane is a saver but also because money holds a lot of meaning for both of them. Jane grew up in a family where there was never enough. She had eight siblings and had to compete with them all the time for any scraps she could get. So, for Jane, having money means that she has security and doesn't have to go without. She feels so anxious whenever she spends money; she feels like she's ten again, not having what she needs. Jane needs to work on this, because she's not at any risk of being without at the moment, but it's also important to respect that there's a reason she feels the way she does.

Bill, on the other hand, was never allowed to buy anything for himself when he was young. Even when he got a part-time job, often his parents would make him turn over his paycheck, not because they were mean but because they wanted to put the money away in savings for him. The result was that once Bill was independent of his parents, he would tend to spend money immediately. Money for Bill represents freedom: not being told what to do. I hope you can see how this doesn't segue well with Jane. Jane is constantly telling Bill what to do with their money and how (and how not) to spend it! This makes Bill feel trapped and like he's a kid again.

If you have an issue with money and finances, conversation number 1 (covered in chapter 6) is going to be really, really important—not just to discuss your common arguments about money but also to discuss why you feel and react the way you do when it comes to money and finances. Once you understand why your partner buys things without telling you or why they hide money, you'll be able to be much more compassionate, even if you want them to change their behavior.

Your conversations and decisions about money will depend on what the issue is between you. The most common issue for couples is when one of you is a spender and one of you is a saver (like Bill and Jane), but saver–saver duos and spender–spender duos also have issues. You might also have differences about what you should spend money on or who should take care of the finances. Here is a list of questions and thoughts that are important to cover as you discuss money and finances:

- Will we share bank accounts or financial accounts?
- If not, how will we decide who pays the bills?
- Who will do the actual paying of bills?
- Which budgeting system will we use?
- Do we want to have a limit on how much each of us can spend without checking in?
- Do we want to have a limit on the types of things we each can buy without checking in?
- How much spending money do we each need each month?

- How much should we spend on different things (eating out, travel, and so on)?
- What financial goals do we agree on?
- How much money is enough?
- If we came into a large amount of money, how would we spend it?
- Which family, friends, or charity will we give money to and why?
- How much do we want to set aside for retirement? What kind of lifestyle do we want in retirement?
- How much and how should we save?
- What are the things we believe are important to save for?

Nowadays, there are also a multitude of apps and programs that provide good budgeting systems. I recommend those where you can both see what is happening at all times, even if only one of you does the actual finances.

In-Laws and Family Issues

One of my favorite books of all time is *Marriage Rules* by Harriet Lerner. She has some great things to say on in-laws and family issues, and she doesn't mince words when she says, "You each need to deal directly with your own parents when they habitually do something at the expense of someone in your household or violate your ground rules," and "Wherever you find a wife and mother-in-law slugging it out, you'll find a son who's not speaking up to either his mother or his wife" (2012, p. 175).

For a multitude of reasons, people often try to control their partner's relationship with their family of origin. If you don't have a good relationship with your family, you're going to expect that your partner will have the same experience; or if you've always gotten along best on your own, you're going to tend to assume your partner can do the same, or at least you're going to want them to do the same, even if the feeling isn't conscious. Sheila didn't consciously want Chad to have a bad relationship with his family, but she didn't necessarily understand his connection or commitment to them, either. There were times when it felt vaguely threatening to her, as if the choice were her or his family (which of course, it wasn't). No one should dictate your relationship with your own family members, although you, of course, can be sensitive to your partner's complaints and insecurities. No one should ever have to choose between their partner and their family.

Depending on what the issues are, there are many ways to deal with family issues and situations. But here are some nonnegotiables:

- Don't expect your partner to be the one to interact with your family. It's your job to schedule and structure visits, make phone calls, and send birthday presents and cards.
- Do decide what amount of time is best to spend with your family, and limit your visits to that amount. If you notice that the first week of vacation goes well and then things start to fall apart, limit future visits to a week!
- Allow your partner to have breaks and escapes from your family. Understand that your partner isn't as comfortable with your family as you are, and probably never will be. If your partner wants to run out for coffee or pop out to the hardware store on their own, encourage them to do it.
- Anticipate difficulties. Most of us know the landmines that exist in our own families, don't we? (I understand that my partner and I have completely different political leanings from my family of origin, so I can anticipate that getting into a long political discussion isn't going to go well.) I'm not saying you should cut off your family or make hard rules about it, but you probably know if your dad is bigoted, or your mom overbearing or your sister disrespectful, for example. It's a conversation that you and your partner can have in advance so you know your plan of attack.

- You can sometimes do things with your family of origin without your partner. If you're someone who just loves to spend a ton of time with your sibling or your parents, consider that some of that time doesn't have to include your partner, if they don't want to come along. My brother and I both really loved first edition books, and would meet once a year at an antiquarian bookfair to spend the entire day wandering through the book aisles and spending ridiculous amounts of money on old, stale books. Now that my brother has passed away, it's one of my fondest memories of spending time with him. I didn't have to worry about anyone else, whether we were taking too long or spending too much. (I did discuss the budget with my partner ahead of time, though!)

In addition, when it comes to family issues, knowing how to set boundaries is extremely important. If you feel you struggle with boundaries, I suggest a great book, *Where to Draw the Line* by Anne Katherine (2000). Basically, a good boundary is set in advance and has natural consequences. Janine and Scott had a problem with his mom snooping in Janine's office when she came to visit. There wasn't anything ultraprivate in there, but Janine felt disrespected every time it happened. Janine wanted to make a rule that Scott's mom couldn't come to stay anymore, but I suggested setting a good boundary instead. In this case, because it was Scott's mom, he called her and said the following:

"Hey Mom, I just wanted you to know that we really love it when you visit us. We can't wait for you to come up in April. I did want to talk to you about one thing: we've noticed that you sometimes go into Janine's office and go through things. Maybe you're just looking for paper or whatever, but we feel uncomfortable with it, so we'd rather you not do that. You can tell us if there's anything that you need while you're here. If this is too much to ask, we'll have to talk about setting some limits during your visits. But I think you'll be okay with this request, and it will be great to see you!"

I want to note a few important things about this boundary. First, Scott is setting it in advance. Again, it's not wise to wait to set a boundary until after someone has crossed it and you're upset. By that time you're mad, and—well, we all know how conversations go when you're already mad! So if you know the boundary that someone is likely to cross, go ahead and have the conversation before it happens. Second, Scott starts and ends with something positive. My grandma called it "making a sandwich": saying something good, then saying the hard part, and then ending with something good. Lastly, there's a consequence for inaction. In this case, it's pretty vague. Scott knows his mom, and he knows that she will most likely be happy to do what he's asking. But if she does violate the boundary, then the consequence will need to be followed.

I once had a client whose family always ended up telling her how to parent when she visited. So she set the boundary: she asked them to stop doing it and said she would have to go home if they didn't stop. The next time she visited, they had just sat down to dinner when her aunt started in on her parenting. Because she'd already told them what the consequence would be, she didn't say a word. She simply got up from the table, picked up her kids and their stuff, and walked out the door. I was so proud of her. But the crazy part of this story is that it happened again the very next time she visited, and again she got up and left. After that, her family stopped telling her how to parent. You might have to stand your ground a couple of times, but I promise you that boundaries work.

Parenting

Parenting can be a great source of conflict for couples. First, we all grew up in different households with very different parenting styles. Those styles worked for some of us and didn't for others. We're probably trying to do exactly what our parents did—or the exact opposite. And our partner is doing the same! Add that to the fact that no one actually knows how to parent before they have a child, and there is no manual. Furthermore, your own kid isn't the same as any other kid on the planet, so even if you did find the perfect parenting book, it might not apply to your particular situation.

I've rarely met a couple who parented exactly the same way. Different styles can turn you into enemies, but they shouldn't! Often, I can see that two different styles may complement each other well, but the couples don't see it. A typical pattern is that one parent is the "bad guy" (the stricter parent) and the other compensates by being the "good guy" (the more lenient parent), and one (or both of them) has a problem with the way the other parent is doing things. What I also often find is that parents tend to share parenting values even if their parenting styles differ. If you can accept that it's okay to have different parenting styles, you can work better as a team. I've had so many couples break up over parenting issues, and guess what? They still have to parent together, but now they're co-parenting, and it is often twice as hard! Splitting up may have been the right decision, but it doesn't solve the problem of having different parenting styles.

Chris and Lillian couldn't work out their parenting differences and ended up divorcing. I was hired as their co-parenting counselor. Lillian had an issue with the corporal punishment that Chris preferred, and she divorced him because she couldn't tolerate him spanking their kids, which is totally understandable. But now that they were divorced and Chris had the kids 50 percent of the time, Lillian had no control over how Chris disciplined the kids. She worried that she wasn't there to comfort them or assess whether or not Chris ever crossed the line into abusive behavior. I was able to help them in co-parenting; it turned out that Chris's parents spanked him, and he just didn't know another way to get the kids to behave. He also had much higher expectations than Lillian when it came to obedience. In the end, we were able to come up with several disciplinary alternatives to spankings and some ways for Chris to adjust his own instincts and gain a more measured perspective on situations in which he felt the kids were being "disobedient." Lillian still didn't like some of the alternative discipline measures, but at least she knew that her kids weren't being spanked when they weren't with her.

My suggestion for parenting differences is to start with your values. What are you wanting to teach your kids? What do you want them to be like as adults? If you agree on the basic values, then the style issues aren't as much of a problem. For example, let's say that your partner and you share a value that your kids should be financially savvy, but your partner's way of doing that is not to give them an allowance but to pay them for work tasks. Your way of doing it is to teach them to have a bank account, budget, and save. Or, let's say you want them to be good team players, and your partner's way of doing that is to sign them up for every sports team, and your way is to work together as a family to do household chores. If you know that your partner's idea of signing your kids up for every team or paying them for chores is in service of the value you share, it's easier to support your partner's choices even if you would choose to do things differently.

It's good to have a plan in place for what values you want your kids to have going into adulthood and what specific things you'd like to do to teach those values. Your partner will be much more supportive of what you're doing with the kids if you're working toward a shared value, so be curious about why your partner thinks certain things are important in parenting. If you and your partner do not share the same parenting values, you can work on this through the two-conversation method presented in chapters 6 and 7, just like any other difference of opinion.

Sex

Sex is another minefield in relationships because the sex we have when we first meet someone isn't the same sex we're having after four kids, menopause, or a multitude of other issues that can change things! Sex at the beginning is usually easy. Generally, people have around the same libido, it's new and exciting, and they're learning about each other and having fun. Later, it's not so easy. Women and men both have multiple hormonal changes monthly and also over a lifetime. It's rare for sexual desire to be equal between partners at all times throughout a long-term marriage or relationship.

First things first: sex is an integral part of a romantic partnership, whether that partnership is a traditional pairing or includes multiple partners. If you were single and you met someone you did not want to have sex with, you would never put them in the relationship bucket; they'd go in the friend bucket or the acquaintance bucket. So, once you're in a long-term relationship, you can't just say "I'm not interested" without fundamentally changing the nature of your relationship. You can change the nature of your relationship, of course, but only if you both agree on it and are satisfied with the outcome. Also, it's important not to judge one person's preferences as "normal" or "good" and the other person's as "abnormal" or "bad." We're all unique individuals, and this includes our sexual proclivities. Just because our own preferences differ from someone else's doesn't make ours wrong or dysfunctional. It's important to resist the urge to diagnose your partner as lacking in some way because they are not like you.

Another real problem is that most of us don't have language around sex or comfort in talking about it. So even if we have pretty good conflict-resolution skills, conflict around sex is supercharged and highly difficult. In addition, unlike family situations where you can go alone, or parenting issues where you can have different styles, sex is something you do together, so you have to have a meeting of the minds when it comes to what is acceptable. And in almost all cases, you can't go anywhere else to get your unmet needs met, so compromise is essential.

The Problem of Differing Desire

In almost every relationship, there's someone with higher desire and someone with lower desire, and this is probably the most common issue couples have. Levels of desire are not always hugely different, but sometimes they are. I ask couples, "In an ideal world, where you are not stressed or worried or tired, and you're attracted to your partner, how many times a week or month would you like to have sex?" If one of them says every day, and the other says once a week, there's a problem, but at least now it's on the table.

Most couples have not even gone this far in talking about the issue. Generally, there will be a gap between what you each consider to be ideal frequency. Is there a midpoint that would be acceptable to both parties? Can the one who is less interested commit to increasing the frequency just a bit? Could the more interested one respect that effort and be satisfied with a little less than ideal? (The exception to this method is that it's important not to ask someone who has been sexually abused to have sex when there is any internal resistance; more on this below.)

The Problem of Differing Preferences

People enjoy different things sexually, and this isn't wrong, but it can really get in the way in relationships. If you know in advance of a relationship that to be happy you're going to need to have sex in public places, then by all means, seek out a partner who feels the same! But most of us develop our preferences over time, and sometimes we want to do certain things that our partner never wants to do, which can be frustrating. Overall, I encourage everyone to try to be playful and experimental in sexual behavior, but there is usually one "absolutely not" kind of activity. It's a bummer if you really want to do something that your partner is never going to do, but there are hundreds—thousands—of different playful sexual activities. You can look for another one that you both like! I encourage you to be open and up front about what you like and what you don't like so that you can discard—together—the things that are not going to work and spend your time finding new and interesting options. Of course, it's possible that an interest you've developed is a deal breaker; you may not be able to move forward in a relationship that does not include a certain activity, and that's okay too. However, that's an easier decision to make if you feel that you and your partner have tried to resolve the situation in every way possible.

The Problem of Not Being Attracted Anymore

Loss of attraction happens sometimes. Two people who were once very attracted to each other are somehow not attracted to each other now. The key here is to find out why. Often, how we are treated outside the bedroom influences how we feel inside the bedroom. If you're disrespectful to your partner all week long and then can't figure out why they say they're not attracted to you, you don't have a sexual issue—you have a respect problem. Change your behavior outside the bedroom, and you will likely see a change inside.

Other times, there's the dicey issue of some physical issue that alters a partner's perception or attraction. Our bodies change over time, and there are many creative ways to keep sexual attraction alive, but if you are truly not attracted to your partner, they deserve to know. At least, then they have a choice: they can understand and accept it, or they can decide that they don't want to be with someone who isn't attracted to them anymore.

One very big issue that crops up here is a history of sexual abuse. If you or your partner has a history of sexual abuse, it is crucial to do some dedicated work on this with a therapist who specializes in this area. Past history of sexual abuse will absolutely influence your future sexual behavior and desire. Both partners need to commit to understanding as much as they can about the past, healing, and what's helpful, so that together they can overcome this heartbreaking trauma.

There are many other sexual issues that can happen in relationships. I particularly like the book *Come As You Are* by Emily Nagoski (2021) on this topic, but there are many other good books. The main challenge here is to have as open a conversation about sex as you would have about any other topic, being curious and seeking clarity and solutions that work for both of you.

Moving Forward

If you are having conflict around any of the topics covered in this chapter, you would approach them using the same two-conversation process that I presented in part 2. The information in this chapter is meant to help you navigate these conversations a little better.

You now have a road map for handling any conflict that comes up in your relationship along with some additional advice on how to resolve some common issues. The next chapter will talk about some ways to include positivity in your relationship. Positivity is an important part of your conflict playbook because you can't have good conflict if you don't have any goodwill to draw from.

CHAPTER 9

Amplifying the Good in Your Relationship

Back in chapter 5, I talked about how you need to invest in your relationship. You need capital to draw from if you're going to have conflict, and continually doing things that add value to your relationship is therefore very helpful. There are some really great books on the topic, but I do want to spend a chapter here giving you some ideas for how to make sizable deposits into your relationship bank account.

Most of the time, when couples come to see me, they don't even want to make deposits anymore. They want to accuse the other person, get me on their side, or prove their partner wrong. Investing in the relationship or having fun times isn't even on their radar. But, I point out to them, sometimes conflict will dissipate solely because you've had so much fun together. After all, if you've just had an amazing time with someone, you're less likely to notice that the garbage hasn't been taken out. You're happy to just do it or at least ask your partner nicely.

I always love asking couples to talk to me about when they first met. Even if they feel really hopeless, most people light up and start telling me about their four-hour phone conversations, long walks on the beach, or slow dancing. There's a certain rhythm to falling in love. Think about your activities in the last week or so. Were they anything like that? People who are falling in love don't lack communication, change into their rattiest sweats as soon as they get home, or have their nose in their phones 24/7. No one falls in love that way! And yet that's what a lot of my couples have been doing, and then they wonder why their relationship feels like a drag.

But you can amplify the good in your relationship right now by investing in three main things: communication, shared experiences, and time. A little bit (or a lot) of laughter helps too.

I can understand if you don't feel like doing these things right now if you're in a conflictual relationship. I didn't feel like going to the park and pushing my kids on the swings when they were little either, but I did it because I loved them and wanted them to be happy! Similarly, you may need to put a little more effort into your relationship than you feel like doing. If you behave how you're authentically feeling right now, it'll be all withdrawals and no deposits. And I hope I've convinced you that you need to make deposits for your relationship to thrive.

I can't tell you how many times I've sat in my office with people who say they can't think of anything fun to do and that when they go out "there's nothing to talk about." They describe themselves as just not romantic or not creative. The interesting thing is, if these couples split, they're on dating sites three months later with plenty of time, plenty of ideas about interesting and romantic things to do, and plenty to say! It's not that they couldn't do these things—it's that they didn't want to. I can't gift you with the "want to." I wish I could, but that part you'll have to supply yourself. But I can give you some ideas for what to do.

Communication

Remember when you fell in love and how your communication was then? When you're feeling very positively toward someone, your communication is curious and gentle. I'll grant you that it's easier to be curious when you don't know anything about someone, but it's not impossible even when you know someone well. I often say that when I see couples who've been together for ten years, their information about each other is usually about nine years old. That's because when we combine our lives, our conversations tend to switch to household tasks, bill paying, schedules, and kids. We stop talking about who we are as people, and our communication becomes practical and dry.

There are a multitude of tools and books you can use to spice up your conversation. To begin with, I recommend somewhat nonsensical ones that don't have weighty emotional material, like conversation card decks or one of the many versions of "Would you rather?" type books. You can then move up to talking about more emotional topics, using books like *4,000 Questions for Getting to Know Anyone and Everyone* (Kipfer 2015). In addition to these ideas, here are some general communication rules, whether you're talking for fun or talking about issues in your lives.

Ask Open-Ended Questions

Asking open-ended questions is fairly straightforward. The reason it's sometimes hard is that we think we already know the answers. When we first meet, we have to ask questions because we don't know each other: "What scares you?" or "What's your mom like?" are natural questions. Open-ended questions, as you can see, are questions that cannot be answered with a yes or a no. So instead of saying "Should we go to that new Mexican restaurant?" you ask, "What kind of food do you feel like tonight?" Or, instead of "Should we put little Johnny in private school?" you ask, "What do you think the pros and cons of private school are for Johnny?" I hope you can see how much more information you can get this way, even if you already think you know the answer.

Use Exploratory Statements

It turns out the magic three words in a relationship are not "I love you"—which is what most people guess they are—but "Tell me more." This is an example of an exploratory statement. Another good one is "Help me understand." Very few people will refuse to talk if you make an exploratory statement, because people love to talk about themselves and what they think!

Make Empathetic Statements, If Possible

I get that you don't always agree with what your partner is saying, but remember, empathy is not the same as agreement. You can say things like "Wow, that's a tough situation" or "That would hurt my feelings too" without agreeing with the rest of the conversation. When someone basically says, "You're making sense" or "I understand what you're saying," don't you want to tell them more? Whereas if someone says, "That's not what happened" or "You're overreacting," you want to tell them a lot less.

Be Attentive and Present

No one wants to talk when they feel like the other person isn't paying attention. This is why it's good to preface talking with "I'd like to talk to you. Is now a good time?" to increase your chances of being attended to. Also, if your partner doesn't ask you, and you're in the middle of something, you can say, "Hang on, this isn't the best time, and I really want to hear what you have to say." Most people are very willing to wait a few minutes if it means that they will be heard more clearly. Once you are having the conversation, I advise muting distractions. We all know how annoying it is to talk to someone who is on their phone, getting text dings, or keeps glancing at the book in their hand. So make eye contact and pay attention. This isn't rocket science, but it's all too easy to get distracted in a conversation. If you must have your phone on for emergency reasons, ask the other person if it's okay to leave it on and say why. If it's not okay, pick another time to talk.

Shared Experiences

Couples often tell me that they don't have anything in common and therefore may not be a good fit. First, I disagree with the premise that you have to have shared interests to be a good match. I've had many couples throughout the years who do not share many interests together and yet have a good relationship. It's true that they do spend significant time apart pursuing their own interests. But when they come back together again, they are interested in the other person's experience and happy to be together.

Even if you had shared interests to start with, those interests would naturally shift and change over time. When you first met, maybe you liked to hike together, go to concerts, or go wine tasting. But then you had kids, a mortgage, and careers, and now you don't have the energy to hike. Maybe one of you plays golf with colleagues now while the other does yoga. Maybe your musical tastes have diverged. People change. But that doesn't mean that you should stop making an effort to find shared experiences, since it's definitely a plus to enjoy things together.

I don't know about you, but if I suddenly find myself with an afternoon free, I can't think of a single thing to do. But if I'm just swamped with work, there are all kinds of things I wish I had time for! It's common: our creativity goes out the door when we're pressured for an answer. For this reason, I like to have my couples make lists of things they would want to do together if they had more time; and this can be a work in progress, something they can add to over time.

EXERCISE: Make a Shared Activities To-Do List

Start to keep your eyes open for things you might like to do. I'm always on the lookout for fun things. Sometimes I find them on Pinterest, in a magazine, or in the Sunday paper. When I see an advertisement for a new place or hear a friend talk about something fun they did, that gets added to the list. As you start to pay attention, begin to make lists of activities you'd like to try to do with your partner. I recommend breaking down the list like this:

- Things we could do if we have an hour
- Things we could do if we have a morning or afternoon
- Things we could do if we have a weekend (or two days)
- Things we could do on vacation
- Things we could do as a family (if you have kids)

This will give you a wide variety of activities, and if each of you keeps a list and you alternate choosing from each other's list, you'll soon be doing lots of things together. It might be wise to allow a veto: you each get one (or however many you decide ahead of time) to opt out of activities that you absolutely never want to do. I can tell you that if my partner wants to skydive, he can do it on his own! But for the most part, try to be open and flexible so you can potentially discover something new.

After each activity, I suggest having a conversation (ask open-ended questions!) about how you each experienced it and whether or not you should keep it on the list to do again. Or you can compile a separate list entitled "Things We Both Enjoy."

Time

I'm telling you right now that if you never spend time together, your relationship will probably not last—and if it does, it won't last happily. Time together is one of the essentials of relationships. And you know this because when you or your friends got into romantic relationships, you disappeared from your friend circle for a while, right? Suddenly no one could reach you because all your time was being spent on your new partner—long phone conversations, all-night chats, dates, going places, vacationing. You simply must spend time together to keep a healthy relationship balance. I suggest thinking of this in terms of daily time, weekly time, and quarterly time.

Daily Time

I know we're all extremely busy, but we do make time for the things we value. You pretty much always make the time to brush your teeth, right? You might make the time to work out, call your mom, take a lunch break, or whatever. Some of the things we do each day are also tied to something else. For example, I remember to take my medication in the morning because I always do it after I brush my teeth. So, the first thing to consider is if you can tie your daily partner time to something that you already do. If you do this, it will more easily become a habit, and you'll be much less likely to forget.

When our kids were little, we'd have dinner as a family each night, and then after dinner was when my kids got to watch a show they loved. They looked forward to it, which meant my partner and I had about twenty to twenty-five minutes to ourselves right after dinner each and every night. Or maybe you'll have time right after you put the kids to bed. Or maybe you work swing shifts, and you can have some time in the morning over coffee. I'm talking about a period of twenty to thirty minutes, which I think is doable for anyone. There's just got to be a way to find twenty minutes a day for your partner.

The purpose of this daily time is to build a "love map" of your partner (Gottman and Silver 2015, p. 50). Because our inner landscape is changing all the time, we need time to explore the territory. Every time my partner and I part in the mornings, we experience new things that affect us. Maybe I heard a news story, or a new song, or something happened to me that my partner doesn't know. So when we get back together, we need to catch up.

Here are some questions you may want to ask during your daily time together:

- What was the hardest part of your day?
- What was the best part?
- What made you feel most productive?
- Did you talk to anyone interesting today?
- What was your biggest distraction today?
- Is there anything you're worried about?
- What do you hope to accomplish tomorrow?
- Is there anything you need from me that would make you feel special?
- What can I do to cheer you on?
- Was there anything that made you laugh today?

This list may inspire you to ask your own questions. As you can see, the point is not to talk about problems or issues. The purpose of your daily time is to enjoy each other! If you have complaints or are upset about something, follow the conflict road map instead. But this daily time is about knowing each other, having a positive conversation, and practicing talking about things other than the practical and scheduling details of your life.

Weekly Time

I know that having a weekly date is an overdone topic. It's something that everyone knows they're supposed to do, but very few people actually do it. A date night is important, especially if you have kids but even if you don't. We relate to each other differently on neutral ground than at home. Again, people who are falling in love might spend some time at home watching movies or whatever, but they also spend a lot of time out and about, having fun.

One of the barriers to weekly dates is that people try to do too much. You don't need to go to the opera or take a day trip. All you really need is a two-hour period together, outside the house, preferably without kids or friends. The other barrier that comes up sometimes is money, such as if you don't have the money to pay for a weekly babysitter. In this case, if you have friends with kids about the same age as yours, I suggest trading date nights: you watch your friends' kids for two hours on Friday night; they watch your kids for two hours on Saturday night. Easy, and the kids get to have playdates!

Also, I don't recommend doing things that discourage interaction or conversation. I love going to the movies, but there's no conversation or interaction going on between us in a movie theater. If we go miniature golfing, bowling, or just sit at a coffee shop for a couple of hours, we're way more likely to feel connected. Some of the types of questions I noted above in the daily time are also good to ask here. Or you can grab a couple of cards from your conversation card deck and bring them along so that you have discussion topics on your date. Try to avoid heavy, problem-based conversation, and use your lists of shared activities for dates if you can.

Quarterly Time

Ideally, all couples would have a quarterly overnight. Not everyone can make this happen, but if you can do it, it will put a lot of deposits in the relationship bank. Again, don't overcomplicate this. When our kids were little, we sometimes went to a hotel in our own town overnight, so we were only a few minutes away if the kids needed us. This place had a pool and a spa facility, so it felt like we were really getting away. Quarterly time doesn't have to be a vacation, that is. You're just looking for an overnight getaway. If you have family nearby, it'll be easier to find sitters, or you can use the same method I outlined for the weekly date, trading time with another couple.

If you have kids, being able to go to bed and know that you aren't going to be awakened during the night is heavenly. Also, there's something about a hotel or resort that encourages romance in a way that your own bedroom might not. I had one couple who liked to pretend they didn't know each other and would meet up in the hotel bar to spice things up! Anything goes, so you can get creative.

If you commit to spending this kind of time and attention on each other, I promise that you'll have much more to draw from when it comes to conflict. And your conflicts will probably be gentler.

A Word About Laughter

Author Ted Cunningham (2020) says in *A Love That Laughs* that you should have a laugh-to-conflict ratio of 100:1. That would be tough! But I agree with him that laughter can cut through a lot of negativity. Laughter releases dopamine, serotonin, and endorphins, making it one of the best drugs there is—with no side effects! It's a natural way to make deposits in your relationship bank. It's really hard to be mad at or hold a grudge against someone whom you regularly laugh with.

How to make more laughter in your lives? First, pay attention to the things that happen in your day. Notice funny things. Have you ever seen a hilarious sign on the road or heard something funny on the radio and maybe you laughed but then forgot all about it? Start paying attention. If you laugh at something funny, note it so you'll remember to tell your partner at the end of the day (or whenever your daily time is). Funny things are happening around us all the time. You might have to lighten up a bit and not take things so seriously all the time so you can notice the humor that already exists around you.

Second, intentionally create things to laugh about. Watching funny shows or movies is an easy way to do this, especially if it's a show you already know you both like. But most of us also scroll through some social media every day, and I can't think of a day when I didn't see anything funny at all. You can do things like play games, have silly dance parties, or intentionally tell a joke to each other every day. Start paying attention, and you'll be surprised by how much more there is to laugh about in the world.

One caveat: the point is to laugh together—and not at your partner's expense. I once saw a family who said they had so much laughter in their house, and yet they were coming to me because their family wasn't working for them. It didn't take me long to understand that the laughter in the home was always at someone's expense. They would say, "We're just joking! Geez, lighten up!" A person knows when you are not joking even if you have a joking tone. We can deeply hurt someone with a joke, and we usually know when we're doing it. We have something we don't want to say, or don't feel safe saying, so we make a joke to make our point. Don't do this, please. If something is bothering you, you now have a conflict road map that will work for you, so have the conversation you really need to have about it. Don't make a joke instead of being brave and having the conversation.

EXERCISE: Make a Plan

It's time to get out your calendars and start making plans. Figure out when your daily time will be, and get it on the calendar. Figure out what the best time for a weekly date is, and schedule it. Plan your first overnight, and when you go, put another one on the calendar for three months away. Start your lists of shared activities so that you'll have some fun ideas when the time comes. Your time can always be rescheduled if something really, really important comes up, but I encourage you to stick to your schedule as much as possible.

I can't stress enough the value of making a plan to spend time with your partner and putting it in your calendars. Personally, if I don't schedule it, it's not going to happen; something else always takes precedence over talking time or a date night, and we figure, "We're fine, we'll do it later."

Spending time with your partner is a good habit to develop, like drinking water: by the time you're thirsty, you should have already been drinking water. If you realize you need to spend more time with your partner, you should have already been doing it!

Moving Forward

I'm guessing at this point you have a bunch of questions that are based on your unique relationship and its challenges. I've tried to imagine what kinds of issues you might run into based on the ways I've seen this process go sideways in my therapy office. The next chapter will focus on troubleshooting some of the most common challenges I see when couples try to follow my road map.

CHAPTER 10

Troubleshooting Your Conflicts

When I walk clients through the conflict process offered in this book, questions will inevitably arise when it doesn't work perfectly. The skill of healthy conflict, like any skill, takes time to develop. Like I said at the beginning, if I gave you a unicycle and told you to go outside and ride, it would take some time before you could do it, and your attempts might involve falls. The answer is not to give up but to keep getting back on the unicycle to try again. This chapter will try to give you a little boost by exploring some issues that might arise as you learn the skill of healthy conflict.

When Your Process "Doesn't Work"

I asked Jessica and Jose how it went when they tried conversation number 1 at home about a small issue. The process "just didn't work," they said.

"What happened?" I asked. "Did you follow the road map?"

"Yes, we followed it," said Jessica.

"So, Jessica, you spoke about how you felt, and Jose repeated it back to you?" I asked.

"Yep," she said.

"Did he do a good job repeating it back?" I asked.

"He did a fairly good job, yes," said Jessica.

"Okay, and then he validated what you said, and you switched so that you could do the same for him?" I asked.

"Oh. No, we didn't do that," said Jessica. "After he repeated back what I said, he started telling me why I was being ridiculous and giving me examples of why what I said was invalid, and these examples were from years ago!"

So they didn't follow the process. This is almost always the case when people tell me that their conversation didn't work. You probably started well enough, so it felt like you did all the steps. But if you were to ask yourself if you did each and every step, you probably would discover that you got offtrack somewhere.

Here are some common areas where things go wrong:

- Going into problem-solving in the first conversation
- One person talking about their responses when they're only supposed to be "repeating back" what their partner said
- Not managing physical or emotional responses, and getting triggered
- Bringing up the past or morphing into a second topic or multiple topics

If you ever think, "This isn't working," read back through the conversations outlined in part 2 to figure out where you're getting offtrack, or have the steps in front of you while you're having these conversations.

When the Fight Can't Wait

As you know, part of the conflict road map is to schedule an appointment for the conflict conversation and have a proper setup. But this isn't always possible. It may be possible a lot more often than people think, but it's still true that it isn't always possible.

If it feels urgent, you need to check in with yourself and ask, *Is this really urgent?* What often happens is that people become angry about something that happened and feel like they need to talk about it right away; they don't want to wait and schedule the conversation. I understand the feeling. Believe me, I get mad as much as the next person, and, boy, is it satisfying to just let it fly right then and there! The problem is—and you know this or you wouldn't be reading this book—releasing your anger in the moment doesn't help to resolve the conflict. I have a lot of clients who say they just want to resolve things immediately. Others say that you should never go to bed mad. But if having things out in the moment, when one or both of you is upset, makes things measurably worse, I'd rather see you wait and resolve the conflict later to the satisfaction of both of you.

If the fight really cannot wait, then you have to learn to do an abbreviated version of your conflict conversations on the fly. Say you are at the car dealer being pressured to buy, and one of you wants to but the other doesn't. Or say one of you has an emergency call to take and suddenly can't do something they've committed to doing. Something has to be worked out, and quickly. In this case, if one decision carries no cost (or less cost), then make that decision if it will buy you time to conduct the conflict conversation later. Using the examples just mentioned, there's not much cost to going home from the dealer, having the conversation later that night, and going back the next day. Or, in the second scenario, you can do the task your partner can't do, even if it inconveniences you, and then follow up with a full conflict conversation later, so you can plan better for similar situations that may arise.

If all else fails, lean heavily on listening and understanding each other quickly so that you can make the decision with lowest impact, and then follow it up later with a full recap of the situation and how it could have gone differently. For example, you could decide that you won't go out to make big purchases in the future unless you've already agreed to the purchase; or you could agree that only certain emergency situations would warrant reneging on your responsibilities.

Over time, if you really follow the conflict road map, you'll get better and better at managing your responses, combining the two conversations into one, and listening to understand. The more you practice, the more the process will feel natural, and you'll be able drop right into it even in emergency situations. These should be few and far between, though, because although it feels good to fight when you're mad, you'll see in practice that it's much more satisfying to wait and reach resolution.

When There Is No Compromise

What happens when one person wants to have a baby and the other doesn't? This is the most common situation when there is no compromise. But it could also be that one person wants to move somewhere and the other person doesn't, or one person wants the kids in private school and the other person wants them in public. In these situations, one person is going to get their way 100 percent and the other person is going to get 0 percent of what they want. Not every situation has a reasonable outcome that satisfies all parties.

Let's look at a situation where one person gets a job offer in a different location and their partner doesn't want to move. This is an emotionally brutal conflict that involves deep-seated desires that people usually have a hard time just discarding. When couples come in with a situation like this, they're typically locked into their two options and haven't really explored anything else. It's more about "I want this and you don't." But if you follow the conflict road map, you can both learn a lot.

Sandy has been given a job opportunity and wants to take it. Her partner, Hakeem, does not want to move. We begin with conversation number 1. First, I seek to understand why the job is important to Sandy, which Hakeem has never really done. What does this job represent? Sandy feels like women are never offered this advancement opportunity in her company, and she wants a chance to break that glass ceiling. I ask Hakeem if it makes sense to him. Hakeem acknowledges that it does but adds that in his culture, it's difficult not to be the breadwinner and that his own career choices will decrease with this move. I ask Sandy if she's thought of that eventuality: what if her success means his failure? I spend a lot of time exploring their feelings and their projections of what might be the outcomes of both the decision to go and the decision to stay. Conversation number 1 brings about a lot of empathy for why they're holding so tightly to each of their positions.

It's true that in the end, one of them will get their way and the other won't. However, they'll be making that decision with greater understanding and empathy now that they've talked about it fully and really heard each other. And they will possibly come up with some alternative solutions in their brainstorming that they wouldn't have considered before. In the end, Sandy and Hakeem decided to make the move so that Sandy could enjoy this success, but they also decided to invest some money into a new business that Hakeem could start, something he'd always dreamed of doing but hadn't had the courage to put into play.

There isn't a downside to approaching the conflict by having these conversations, even if ultimately one person will get their way. You'll understand each other better, empathize with what's underneath the choice, and maybe come up with some really creative solutions so both of you will feel good about the decision.

When You're Doing This on Your Own

Clearly, things will go better if both halves of a couple are reading this book and taking in all the concepts here. But you may be the only one reading this book to improve things. Again, that's okay. I do believe that one person can change a relationship single-handedly—maybe not to their full satisfaction—but if one of you does something different, the other person cannot stay exactly the same. If your partner doesn't cooperate with this process, and continues to blow up at you when they get mad, you can still take measures to improve things, which I hope I've done a good job of explaining throughout. Here are some of your options:

- You can try to schedule conversations when you're the one who is mad and you want to discuss a problem. Your partner may not ask to schedule a conversation when they're the one who is mad, but you can schedule it for them. This at least ensures that your partner doesn't start the conversation angry. They also might respond better, since you let them choose the time and they know the topic. They aren't getting ambushed or being faced with an angry you, and that can only help.
- You can still stick to one topic, manage your own physical and emotional responses, and try to loosely follow the understanding-before-solutions road map. If your partner goes straight into solutions, for example, you can say, "Before we talk about what to do, I really, really want to understand more about what you're thinking."
- If your partner is the one who's mad and goes straight into an argument, you can refuse to respond in kind. You can seek to ask curious questions and understand where they're coming from. A side benefit to this may be that they then want to know and understand you, but you can't count on it. Still, your desire to understand your partner is likely to bring the emotional temperature down a notch and help extinguish the anger.

I should say that there are some people you may never be able to have healthy conflict with. There are certain issues that make it extremely difficult to manage conflict: substance abuse, conflict avoidance, certain personalities, or untreated mental health conditions can make it difficult to have calm, reasonable conversations. It's not impossible. Again, seeking to be calm and understanding can only help, and all of these issues are ones in which treatment is possible and reachable.

On the other hand, with partners who are truly antisocial or narcissistic, there might be no chance to learn the skill of conflict. These disorders are on a spectrum, and those on the lower end may have little to no trouble learning healthy conflict if they're dedicated to learning, so don't discount a partner who is simply introverted, reclusive, or self-absorbed. However, a fully diagnosed antisocial or narcissistic personality disordered person will not be able to tolerate the method of conflict resolution outlined in this book, because someone with antisocial personality disorder simply does not care about anyone else's viewpoint, and those with narcissistic personality disorder lack empathy. If you're in a relationship with this sort of person, I suggest educating yourself with the numerous resources on these disorders or joining a local support group such as NAMI (National Alliance on Mental Illness). You can still always change yourself and, with support, may be able to stay in the relationship and thrive. Every situation is different.

Again, even with people who cannot do this process, you can still manage you. You can monitor your own physical and emotional responses and stay calm throughout the discussion. You can still seek to understand and empathize even though your partner will not be able to return the favor. But you may not be able to collaborate on a joint process.

When You "Can't Manage" Your Anger

Some people say they can't manage their own anger. They say that in their experience, there's no space between whatever triggers them and their response. But I don't buy it. I ask, "Have you ever wanted to swear at your boss?" or "Have you ever been so mad while driving, you wanted to run someone off the road?" The answer to both of these questions is usually yes. Then I ask, "Well? Did you actually do it?" and the answer is always no. Why? Because doing these things would bring some very heavy consequences that most of us aren't willing to pay. We'd get fired or we would go to jail.

The consequences of anger with our partner also exist, but they are not as immediate as those examples. Exploding at our partner is more like how we may behave with food. Yeah, I know the consequences of eating ice cream every day is weight gain, but on any particular day, I can pretend I don't know that, so I can have ice cream. We all know, however, that certain consequences will come to pass if we behave this way long enough.

It's clear that we can manage our anger; there are many, many situations on a regular basis where we don't just go off, however much we may want to. It's more likely that with our partners, we don't want to manage our anger. I do agree that this area—our closest relationships—is much more challenging to manage than other situations. But I still believe that it can be done with effort.

The key here is to widen the gap between the trigger and your response. A quote widely attributed to Victor Frankl (but which appears to be by Rollo May from his 1963 article "Freedom and Responsibility Re-examined") says, "Between stimulus and response there is a space. In that space is our power to choose our response. In our response lies our growth and our freedom." Even a few seconds of time between those things can help you make a decision about how you want to respond so you don't just react. How can you get those few seconds? Look again at chapter 4 on managing your bodily responses. And before you say, "I've tried that," ask yourself how consistently you're practicing. You will not be able to behave with calm in an upsetting situation if you never practice these responses when you're feeling calm. You must be practicing mindfulness, breathing, or whatever your favorite methods are on a daily basis if you want to be able to access them when you're mad.

Additionally, there is some usefulness to tapping in to your values. What kind of a person do you want to be? How badly do you want that? Does creating a gap to choose your response have greater value than just reacting to whatever happens? If your desire to behave better is just a vague, ethereal goal, you will not be able to grab onto that goal when something makes you mad, however. You might want to really flesh out, in writing, the benefits of having a more measured response and why you want to do this in your life. If all else fails, most communities have anger management groups or classes that will encourage you to practice techniques on a regular basis in the presence of others.

When You Mess Up

Obviously, you're going to mess up. You're going to get this wrong and get offtrack. That's just the nature of learning something new, and also the nature of anger and conflict. Again, this is a skill, and as such, there is a learning curve and process. Also, it's a practice, and it's easy to think "I've got a handle on this now," and then stop practicing your daily breathing or mindfulness, or to start thinking you don't need some of the steps I've presented. There will also be times when your anger just feels out of your control and perhaps even out of proportion to what is happening. Maybe you're exhausted or you let yourself get too hungry. Whatever the issue is, you're going to screw this up sometimes.

No problem! The beauty of learning is that a bad day has a lot to teach us. I used to be an air traffic controller, and when I trained other controllers and they made no mistakes, I would always say, "Well, that was a waste of a day!" Of course, they thought it was an amazing day, but we aren't learning anything when we're doing everything right all the time. There is nothing like messing something up to really teach us something.

Hopefully, when this inevitably happens, the two of you will be on the same page and realize that you both messed up. But even if not, one of you can say, "Wow, that really didn't go well last night. Can we talk about what went wrong?" This conversation is not a topical conversation; this isn't just a rerun of the conversation that didn't go well. You might need to do that, too, but first you want to have what we call a *process* conversation, a conversation about the process you went through and where it went wrong. You may have to touch on content here, like "When you said I was rude, I really lost it," but the content isn't the point. The point is to figure out where you got offtrack, so it can be corrected.

Running back through all of the steps—maybe even having them in front of you in written form—will help. You can ask, "Did we do this?" "Did we start here?" "Did we do the steps in order?" As you're discussing it, figure out where things went sideways. Should you have called a time-out? Did you need to take a breath? Did you feel compelled to throw in another topic?

Once you understand the points in the conversation where things went wrong, try to come up with solutions that will address those things in the future. Was there a feeling you had in your body right before it happened? You might need to say, "When I feel my stomach drop like that, I know I need a time-out" or "I definitely need a notepad in front of me so I can write down other topics that come to mind."

Try to be gentle and compassionate toward each other as you discuss what went wrong. You're not enemies; you're just trying really hard to learn something new! End this conversation with some sort of acknowledgment of how hard you are both trying and with the confidence that you'll get it eventually.

When There's Too Much Water Under the Bridge

A stunning statistic is that couples wait an average of six years after realizing they have serious problems to seek help (Gottman and Silver 2015). By this time, there's so much history and so much hurt that any conflict conversation is fraught with difficulty.

You won't be surprised to know that I think that goodwill deposits are the place to begin. It is imperative that you have something to draw from if you are going to have any type of healthy conflict. I understand that this is not easy when you're distressed as a couple, but if you begin with some enjoyable activities, it will help immensely. Bonding hormones are released when people adventure together, so you're creating connection even if it's against your will!

Next, it will be very difficult when following the road map to stick with one topic at a time or to start small. It will seem like there are so many pressing items, so many tragic differences; how can you possibly just discuss the issue last week with little Johnny? Every conversation degenerates into a litany of every bad thing that your partner has ever said or done.

You can't let go of the past if it's still happening. In other words, I don't ask my clients to just forget what has happened if it is still happening! For this reason, I suggest starting with the most recent issue and working backwards. As you repair your current issues, and your current partnership starts to work better (and you're doing fun things together), it will become easier and easier to process through the old hurts. Sometimes it may not even be necessary to process through an old hurt if that pattern has been repaired in the current day.

There's probably no end to the possible questions that you'll have regarding this road map. Every couple is unique and has a different set of personalities, temperaments, and issues. I believe that my conflict road map can assist you in any conflict that you are having, but you may also need to apply your own creative ideas and inspiration to the process.

CHAPTER 11

Summary and Wrap-Up

We've reached the end of our journey together, and I sure hope that you've learned something valuable from this book. My passion in life is helping couples navigate the difficulties of relationships so that we can have more stable couples and families. Conflict management is an integral part of that process, because conflict ensures that two different and separate people can feel heard and understood, and options can be created and considered that work for both parties.

My parting advice is to work on your own part of the equation, and to keep trying and never give up on becoming more skilled at conflict. This road can be hurtful and discouraging at times, and it's tempting to think that it might be easier to just give up and start over. We know by now that this just isn't true. Divorce and separation, while sometimes absolutely necessary, are not easy by any means. In addition, getting divorced or separating does not alleviate the need for constructive conflict, both with your ex-partner and your future ones. Relationships are where we learn about ourselves and others, and it is often not easy. But it's worth it.

You can't control anyone else. You can't control their feelings or their behavior. The only person you have agency over is yourself. That's why the most important thing you can do is practice these concepts yourself, in all of your relationships, if you want to see real change. There are many things in this book that you can do independently, not the least of which is to develop a daily practice that helps you stay calm and manage your responses. I hope you can see that this skill will serve you well not only in your romantic relationships but in almost every situation you find yourself in. Developing it is a daily practice; it does not work as an occasional endeavor. If this is the only thing you do after reading this book, I still think that you'll see changes in your life and relationships that will astound you.

Also, a commitment to keep trying and not give up is useful. Not that you should never give up on any relationship; sometimes relationships are not viable and do run their course. But it's important to commit to the process. If you're already in a severely damaged relationship, it's true that this process might not resolve and heal everything. But the process itself is still valuable, and you can put it to use in your future relationships and any other nonromantic current relationships. Slowing things down, seeking understanding, finding multiple options, and going back over things that didn't go right will never steer you wrong. Don't view healthy conflict as being successful or unsuccessful; just view it as a practice that you are always refining.

I'm cheering you on from the sidelines and hoping that this process will improve your relationship with yourself and others.

Acknowledgments

Books are just thoughts and ideas until an editor comes along who believes in them. I've spent years expressing these ideas to couples one-on-one, never thinking that I could have a wider audience. I owe a huge debt of gratitude to my editor Georgia Kolias at New Harbinger, who saw something in this manuscript worth sharing with the world. There is no way this book would be even close to what you are holding in your hands without Georgia's unending support and help.

I am also so thankful for the editing and help given by Vicraj Gill, Madison Davis, and Brady Kahn, along with the entire team at New Harbinger.

I'm grateful for the years of encouragement by my colleagues who have badgered and nagged me to write down my thoughts, and am particularly grateful for the longstanding support and multiple rough-draft readings by Lauralee Ragsdale and Jeannie Wolitzer. You guys are the best!

My best friend Lisa has been a tireless support, willingly reading every draft and revision and giving me her wise reactions to and thoughts about my ideas. I could not do life without you!

Thank you to my son Ethan, an amazing animator, who did the original illustrations for this book. I hope you and your brother Quinlan learn good conflict skills, even if you have to read a book by your mom!

And of course, I am so very thankful to my husband Tom, without whom I wouldn't even be a therapist and therefore would have none of this to share with the world. Thanks for being supportive of every crazy idea I've had!

References

Cunningham, T. 2020. *A Love That Laughs: Lighten Up, Cut Loose, and Enjoy Life Together.* Carol Stream, IL: Tyndale House Publishers.

Engel, B. 2020. *Escaping Emotional Abuse: Healing from the Shame You Don't Deserve.* New York: Citadel Press.

Fisher, R., W. Ury, and B. Patton. 2011. *Getting to Yes: Negotiating Agreement Without Giving In.* 3rd ed. New York: Penguin Books.

Gottman, J., and N. Silver. 2015. *The Seven Principles for Making Marriage Work: A Practical Guide from the Country's Foremost Relationship Expert.* 2nd ed. New York: Harmony Books.

Hanson, R. 2009. *Buddha's Brain: The Practical Neuroscience of Happiness, Love, and Wisdom.* Oakland, CA: New Harbinger Publications.

Katherine, A. 2000. *Where to Draw the Line: How to Set Healthy Boundaries Every Day.* New York: Fireside Books.

Kipfer, B. A. 2015. *4000 Questions for Getting to Know Anyone and Everyone.* 2nd ed. New York: Random House Reference.

Lerner, H. 2012. *Marriage Rules: A Manual for the Married and the Coupled Up.* New York: Gotham Books.

Nagoski, E. 2021. *Come As You Are: The Surprising New Science That Will Transform Your Sex Life*. Revised and updated ed. New York: Simon and Schuster.

Porges, S. 2011. *The Polyvagal Theory: Neurophysiological Foundations of Emotions, Attachment, Communication, and Self-Regulation* (Norton Series on Interpersonal Neurobiology). 1st ed. New York: W. W. Norton and Company.

Siegel, D. J. 2020. *The Developing Mind: How Relationships and the Brain Interact to Shape Who We Are*. 3rd ed. New York: Guilford Press.

Siegel, M. 2018. "The Fallibility of Memory." *The Hill*. October 4. https://thehill.com/opinion/healthcare/409945-the-fallibility-of-memory.

Tatkin, S. 2012. *Wired for Love: How Understanding Your Partner's Brain and Attachment Style Can Help You Defuse Conflict and Build a Secure Relationship*. Oakland, CA: New Harbinger Publications.

Vernick, L. 2013. *The Emotionally Destructive Marriage: How to Find Your Voice and Reclaim Your Hope*. Colorado Springs: Waterbrook Books.

Wile, D. 1995. *After the Fight: Using Your Disagreements to Build a Stronger Relationship*. New York: Guilford Press.

Lisa Gray, LMFT, is a licensed mental health professional with a private practice in the San Francisco Bay Area, where she specializes in high-conflict couples and chronic illness/pain. After working as an air traffic controller for ten years, and serving as a peer debriefing counselor for fellow controllers, Lisa decided to go back to school to study counseling. She graduated from John F. Kennedy University in 2004 with a master's degree in clinical counseling, and has been working in the field ever since. Lisa is passionate about teaching couples to practice healthy conflict, so that their relationships can thrive and grow. Lisa reviews self-help books on her Instagram, Therapy Book Nook. She lives in the Bay Area with her family and three large dogs.

Did you know there are **free tools** you can download for this book?

Free tools are things like **worksheets**, **guided meditation exercises**, and **more** that will help you get the most out of your book.

You can download free tools for this book—whether you bought or borrowed it, in any format, from any source—from the New Harbinger website. All you need is a NewHarbinger.com account. Just use the URL provided in this book to view the free tools that are available for it. Then, click on the "download" button for the free tool you want, and follow the prompts that appear to log in to your NewHarbinger.com account and download the material.

You can also save the free tools for this book to your **Free Tools Library** so you can access them again anytime, just by logging in to your account! Just look for this button on the book's free tools page.

+ Save this to my free tools library

If you need help accessing or downloading free tools, visit **newharbinger.com/faq** or contact us at **customerservice@newharbinger.com.**